INSIDE (

Edited by Stephen Oliver

First published in Great Britain in 2013

Society for Promoting Christian Knowledge
36 Causton Street
London SW1P 4ST
www.spckpublishing.co.uk

British Library Cataloguing-in-Publication Data
A catalogue record for this book is available from the British Library

ISBN 978–0–281–06843–2
eBook ISBN 978–0–281–06844–9

Typeset by Graphicraft Limited, Hong Kong
First printed in Great Britain by Ashford Colour Press
Subsequently digitally printed in Great Britain

Produced on paper from sustainable forests

*In honour of Barbara, David, Esther, Hilary,
Kevin, Muriel, Rachael, Roland, Rosina and Roy*

My grief lies all within. And these external manners of lament are merely shadows to the unseen grief that swells with silence in the tortured soul.
(William Shakespeare, *Richard II*, Act IV)

Contents

Contributors

Rabbi Howard Cooper is a rabbinic graduate of Leo Baeck College, London and a psychoanalytic psychotherapist in private practice. He works part time as Director of Spiritual Development at Finchley Reform Synagogue and is the author of *The Alphabet of Paradise: An A–Z of Spirituality for Everyday Life*.

Professor Pat Jalland has been a Professor of History at the Australian National University since 1997. She is the author of nine books, including *Death in War and Peace: A History of Loss and Grief in England, 1914–1970* (Oxford University Press, 2012).

Dr Jonathan Martin is a consultant in palliative medicine at St Joseph's Hospice, London and Visiting Fellow at Harris Manchester College, Oxford University. He worked in academic general practice before training in palliative medicine in 2004. He is engaged in research and developing the role of palliative care for patients with chronic respiratory disease.

The Rt Revd Stephen Oliver was Chief Producer of religious programmes at the BBC before becoming Canon Precentor of St Paul's Cathedral, London. From 2003 to 2010 he was Bishop of Stepney in east London.

The Revd Jennifer Replogle is Curate at Trinity Church, Princeton, New Jersey and a graduate of Princeton Theological Seminary.

The Revd Ben Rhodes is an Anglican priest, Spiritual Care Lead and Chaplaincy Team Manager at King's College Hospital NHS Foundation Trust, London. Ben has worked in the NHS for over 12 years in hospitals in east and south-east London.

Mary Slevin was born in London, trained as a nurse in Hackney and worked in the acute sector until after the birth of her children. Following the death of her husband she trained as a health visitor. She moved into clinical, then general management, ending her career as a chief executive nurse. She is a trained Cruse volunteer and lives in Hertfordshire.

The Revd Richard M. Smith CF is a Methodist minister and joined the Royal Army Chaplains department in 2003. He has completed tours in Iraq and Afghanistan. At the time of writing he continues to serve at Catterick Garrison in North Yorkshire.

Dr Sue Smith is a clinical psychologist practising in the London Borough of Tower Hamlets. She provides psychology support for people with life-limiting conditions and those close to them, as well as to her fellow health professionals.

Foreword

ROWAN WILLIAMS

The key word in this book's title is 'inside'. This is not meant to be a brisk and useful book on coping; it is a record, in various ways, of the experience of inhabiting grief. This doesn't mean that it is a plain record of unrelieved pain, though there is plenty of that in these pages: 'inhabiting' grief is a matter of learning a landscape, recognizing an environment in which you are going to live for a long time, probably a lifetime. That's why more than one of these pieces is sceptical about the language of 'closure', and why again and again the writers underline the risks of importing solutions, even the most well-meaning and well-grounded, from outside without paying attention to the actual rhythms of grief as lived in (not lived through and left behind).

The title of Stephen Oliver's opening essay sets the tone of what follows: 'No one ever told me.' Echoing the beginning of C. S. Lewis's devastating self-analysis in *A Grief Observed*, this reflection touches on a wide range of utterly unexpected elements in bereavement. In a very paradoxical way, this book is not trying to 'tell' us things that will then help us manage our own grief better, but alerting us to the human depth and difference of the experiences people live in. No one will or can ever, in that sense, *tell* us. However much you may think that exposure to other people's grief might prepare you for your own tragedies, it doesn't work like that; and, as Jennifer Replogle underlines, the delayed impact of personal loss on someone who has professionally to support others through it is a significant and overlooked issue. But at the same time, more than one of these pieces (particularly the chapter by Sue Smith and Jon Martin) reminds us that the impact of death on carers and accompaniers is more complex and troubling than we might like to think. They too have to 'inhabit' uncontrollable and unexpected territory and need to be supported in their own challenges and solitudes.

It is sobering to read some of the catalogues (like that offered by Mary Slevin) of the clichés that spring readily to the lips of some, especially religious, people; and illuminating to trace with Pat Jalland the ins and outs of what is culturally usual and acceptable in grieving. There are no timeless right answers to be found; and awareness of the cultural and religious diversity of our society shows us how diverse the rituals are that allow people to make what sense they can of their grief. Ben Rhodes gently points out some of the pitfalls that may open up when such awareness is lacking; and Howard Cooper offers a richly three-dimensional picture of aspects of grieving in Jewish communities, highlighting the way in which this context makes the process something that is *shared* in ways that are now unusual to most of us. Richard Smith's account of the rituals of death and mourning in the armed forces reminds us of how violent death in foreign war has come once again to be a regular aspect of people's experience in the UK, in a way largely unknown in the four decades before the 1990s. It is moving to hear about the improvising of rituals – and disturbing also to think about the inescapable pressures that seem to leave so little time and space for the handling of this traumatic kind of loss. We need to be aware of the scale of what we ask of servicemen and women.

All in all, this is a particularly 'open' book – open in its candour and rawness about the unfinished and unfinishable business of grieving, open in its refusal to turn away from the not-knowing and impotence that attend the experiences described. If we are to find words of faith to speak in the presence of loss, they have to emerge from whatever we can do to inhabit the territory alongside those who are grieving, to move as far inside as we can; and for Christians that is entirely consistent with their central belief in God who heals only by inhabiting the world of death and grief.

Preface

STEPHEN OLIVER

It is fifty years since C. S. Lewis published his deeply personal, raw and revealing account of *A Grief Observed.*

The intervening decades have seen the expansion of the modern hospice movement and the production of successive studies in the psychodynamics of grief. Death is not quite the unmentionable topic it once was, but grief still remains a tricky subject for conversation. In one sense that is hardly a surprise. Few people in their all-consuming grief can articulate what they feel. In truth grief is, in itself, way beyond words.

Yet for those around the one experiencing the rawness of grief, her family, friends, neighbours and colleagues, this can be a bewildering time. These often struggle to understand what is going on inside the one they care for, and at the same time are afraid to say or do the wrong thing. They become wary of triggering painful memories and can be embarrassed, even frightened by cascading tears and overwhelming emotion.

It is our hope that in this book those in the grip of primary grief will recognize some familiar features of the landscape, and that those around them will gain some small access to what it feels like to be inside grief, albeit with the proviso that the experience of each person is unique. More than that, we hope that this book will give them sufficient insight not to be afraid of grief and to have the confidence to maintain contact with the one they care about. Words are not necessary. Contact is crucial.

I believe that this is particularly important where grief follows traumatic death or a prolonged and exhausting period of care during a devastating illness. Often the grieving person can find himself, unwittingly, isolated and alone. It is all too easy for everyone to assume that someone else will be keeping contact with him. Without the mourning rituals and social conventions of past ages, it becomes even more important that those in deep bereavement are given sensitive care and support even when they deny any need for it.

I am deeply grateful to those who have contributed to this book their rich experience, skill and wisdom. It is not without considerable personal cost in knowledge and deep reflection that these pages have been written. Particular thanks go to Carrie Geddes, who collated the chapters with such professional expertise and calm efficiency.

Finally, this book is offered in honour of those to whom its chapters are dedicated, whether named or unnamed; those who, more than the memory of their death, have taught us to treasure the gift of their life.

1

No one ever told me

STEPHEN OLIVER

No one ever told me that grief is so visceral and so voracious in its capacity to consume memory, confidence and concentration. This in itself came as a profound surprise. I have worked in hospices alongside some of the finest doctors and nurses. In my professional life I have tried to give support to those enduring the painful loss of a husband, wife or child. Yet I now realize just how little I understood. In retrospect I suppose it is always like that when what you know in your head becomes the indescribable hole in your heart.

I was attending a conference in France when H called. We had met as teenagers and been married for over forty years. H was a distinguished and dedicated nurse. Now a routine examination had revealed a sinister shadow on her pancreas. We both knew immediately what the significance of that might be and fortunately had always been able to talk openly, honestly and gently of important things. In that sense, though painful, this was no different. Yet I still look back with wonder at the enormous courage with which H discussed the implications of her diagnosis and the determination with which she was to endure the treatment that followed. From that moment there was never a morning that I did not wake without a sense of dread, not unlike fear, buried within the gnawing hole I felt in my gut. Then and now I would gladly and gratefully have given anything for it to be me and not her. Grief, I now understand, was already the unseen stalking companion on the road that lay ahead.

Major surgery was quickly followed by intensive chemo-therapy. The side effects of cumulative sickness and exhaustion grew more severe as the treatment went on. Then it became increasingly difficult and stressful for the nurses to get into a vein in order to take blood or administer drugs. Sometimes, it was such an overwhelming relief when the needle went in first time that I openly wept. More often it would take several painful attempts and that proved distressing, not least to the nurses who were using every ounce of their considerable skill. Finally, we paid to have a 'port-a-cath' inserted under the skin to give more permanent access for delivering medication. It was the best money we ever spent.

The very nature of this cancer meant that we knew the treat-ment was buying time but probably would not greatly extend H's life. We learned, at last, the hard but liberating lesson to live each day for itself. This became even more important after H decided with her wise doctor that the chemotherapy was no longer effective and the time had come to stop any further treatment. We made the most of what little time was left. H gradually became weaker and noticeably jaundiced; there were times of mental confusion, extended bouts of nausea and increased pain that proved difficult to control at home.

The time came, as we had planned, to leave our home together for the last time. Both of us had worked in hospice care and were grateful that such care was there for us now. These were important days. H wanted to plan her funeral with me, and some found it strange that it was done so far in advance and that we did it together. It was not achieved without many tears for both of us. It was one of the ways in which we were able to say goodbye. Grief was no longer the unseen companion on the journey but an increasingly forceful presence. H spent an afternoon looking through her modest jewellery and deciding who was to be given each item as a final gift from her. Though her body was failing, H became to my eyes more radiant and more beautiful in a way that I still find impossible to describe.

Yet no one knows how hard these days became, as physical symptoms grew worse and gradually H withdrew from the concerns of this world. We were both profoundly grateful for the presence of close family and the gentle support of doctors and nurses and staff around us. By now H was in her bed all the time and I slept fitfully in her room. Some suggested that the end, when it came, would be a relief. But I knew that it is never like that.

One early afternoon I detected a change in her breathing. I was quietly reading aloud some of the psalms we had come to love for their forthright honesty and deep spirituality. I was holding her hand when she took her last breath. Nothing can prepare you for that final moment when the terrible, over-whelming truth and the deep dread of past months come together in such piercing pain and, paradoxically, a mind-numbing nemesis.

Then came what some have described as the gift and grace of tears. The convulsive, body-racking, uncontrollable flood. Anguish and lament. Sorrow and soundless scream. Protest and passion. If I struggle now to find appropriate words it is probably because there are no adequate words to convey this moment. I think of that picture by the Norwegian artist Edvard Munch showing a figure with head in hands and an agonized face set against the tumult of a red sky. The original German title given to this work by Munch can be translated as *The Scream of Nature*. Though I was incapable of describing it at the time, there was nonetheless a deep sense that it was not my personal grief alone that silently screamed in protest at the moment H died. The hole that had so long been in my gut became the raw, inconsolable hole in my heart. Stalking grief was now within.

The days after remain a blur in my mind. Alarmingly, I had no memory of H other than her last days in that hospice bed, and now could barely picture her face in my mind. It was as if memory itself had been washed away. Practical things had to be done and decisions made. In some ways these proved a distraction, yet in other ways it was all surreal. I knew that in every conceivable way I was exhausted, and I had to remind myself that I was not the only one grieving for H. There was a growing torpor, and a heaviness like wading through deep water. Everything appeared to move in slow motion.

So to the funeral. It was her funeral, as she had planned it with me. A lot of people came and I was glad to be surrounded by close family and friends, even if I could not say much – or at least say anything that made sense. Many travelled far that day and all of them in their own way represented different chapters of our life together. Then, at last, I found myself alone.

Many have described how weird it is to be surrounded by people one minute and then find yourself alone the next. In the days to come letters will dry up and telephone calls become fewer. I find I am a mass of contradictions. If I am with people I want to be at home alone. If I am at home I find myself wondering why nobody comes. At first I thought that people found my raw emotions, rolling tears and evident pain too much to bear. Perhaps they did. Yet I now believe that on top of that, people found it hard to handle their own sense of helplessness. In a world where we delude ourselves that everything can be fixed, it comes as something of a surprise to find suddenly that some things cannot be fixed and some things simply cannot be made better.

A few people called for a jolly chat, no doubt with the good intention of cheering me up. My response was pretty monosyllabic if the truth be told. No one can talk me out of grief and no one can make the pain go away, for the simple reason that I do not want my pain taken away. It is the last vestige of love in a different form. If there was no love, there would be little pain. Regret? Perhaps. A passing sadness? Maybe. But the price paid for loving deeply is the unavoidable pain and anguish of grief.

In all this I know that the people who helped most were those who had the great courage to stick with me, bearing my grunts and tears and lack of chat. Courage, because I was sending signals that I wanted to be left alone. Courage, because they knew the risk of rejection: I did not feel anger as most would understand it, but I was intolerant of those who came too close. Courage, because these were the ones who knew that they had no easy solace to give me. Those who told me it would get easier with time, that it would get better, simply did not understand that I did not want it to get easier, and there is no way I would say even now that it gets 'better'. Such condolences I did not find helpful, for they seemed not to take seriously what H had endured nor how desperate was the depth of anguish in my whole being. The ones who were most supportive were those with courage simply to be silent when presence was important but words were not. The best were those brave people who would regularly, but not necessarily frequently, drop me a note or call on the telephone just for a few moments, simply to touch base. They were the ones who flatly refused to abandon me to my isolation. When the time came, and it was after a long time, that I finally had the energy to emerge into the world again, then it was these people who were still there, still in touch. Others had largely disappeared. For those who clearly did not understand anything, I felt on occasion that I had to put on a front, though I had little energy or desire for it. There was only so much others could bear. I felt like the comic who goes on stage even while screaming inside. I wanted to wear a shirt with words printed on the front, 'I'm OK, thank you for asking!' But printed on the back, 'I'm hurting like hell!'

There is no doubt that people cope, or do not cope, with grief in different ways. Shortly after the funeral I went to stay with friends for a few days. In truth it was too early for me as I spent the whole time wishing to be at home, alone. But when I finally left I realized that H had not been mentioned once in conversation. It was as if for my friends H had never been. Although I was upset by it at the time, I now believe that this was a generational difference. My friends had gone through the war years, when loss of family and friends was common. No one was encouraged to do anything but leave the past behind and carry on. For me it simply reinforced the agonizingly empty void. With those sensitive and sensible enough to ask whether I wanted to talk about H, for the most part, I was only too glad to do so.

These were early days, and because no one had told me, I was still unprepared for the sheer physical onslaught of what was to come. Grief does not necessarily begin with death. I was more exhausted than I realized. It had been a long road already and my body began to protest in ways that I found quite frightening. Some days my hand would shake so much that if I picked up a pen I could barely write. My signature changed, which caused a problem or two with the bank. I remember standing at the top of the stairs and my legs would not move, and when they did I had the overwhelming feeling that I would fall. I was no longer in control of my limbs. Even when talking my mouth would feel somehow disconnected and I found it difficult to form words. Brain and voice seemed no longer synchronized. I would fall asleep at odd times, and especially in the evening. Then I would wake in the small hours and restlessly only sleep again in brief snatches. I became accident-prone. A cup would be dropped or a glass knocked over with disturbing regularity. Fortunately, I had a good and kind doctor who was not fazed by my tears and gave me generously of his time. He would examine each new symptom and carefully check me out. On occasion he would call in to see me and to listen. He did once suggest I might be referred to a neurologist, though I suspect that was more to calm my growing anxiety than out of clinical necessity.

More worrying still was the unnerving experience of having panic attacks while driving. It would usually happen if I was overtaking a lorry on a busy motorway with fast traffic all around, or on one occasion feeling out of control as I drove down a steep winding hill with a truck coming down behind me. Often

I would have to pull over and take quite some time to let it subside before carrying on. It was very frightening and I wonder now if I should have been driving at all. No one had told me.

Each time I left my doctor he would ask if I was safe. I knew he was asking whether I was suicidal. I do not think I was suicidal, and except for one bleak day I was able to reassure him I would do nothing stupid. That does not mean I did not think about it, even going so far as to do some pretty serious research. Two convictions finally turned me away from that prospect. I could find no way of ending it all without causing even more pain and distress to others, and especially those closest to me. I also knew that to take my own life when H had hers taken from her would have been the deepest betrayal of all that she believed and all that she had so painfully endured. And she would have been furious with me. My life was ultimately not mine to end. Yet even that is not quite so straightforward. In coming months I would take up some challenging, risky and downright dangerous activities: enough for one friend to say that my life had taken on the character of Russian roulette. I was not suicidal, but death would not have been unwelcome.

A little while ago I read about the presenting physical symptoms of soldiers suffering 'shell shock' in the First World War. Uncannily, my physical response in grief was very similar. I think that what I experienced was a toxic mixture of deep trauma underneath the emerging conscious grief that was released when H died. Watching the one you love most go through so much, and over a relatively long and intense time, is profoundly traumatic, and is probably made worse by the fact that much has to be suppressed simply in order to cope with what is happening day by day. I was sometimes asked how I was doing. The simple answer was that I did not know. For quite some time it had taken everything I had to care for H and continue to cope, as best I could, with the responsibilities of my work. There was simply nothing left over for any kind of personal introspection.

If the sheer visceral effect of grief on my body came as a surprise, then the complex mental lethargy was even more of a shock. No one ever told me how weird that would be. I felt at times I was losing my mind. I found I could not concentrate on anything. I love to read, but I could only manage a couple of paragraphs before my mind went walkabout somewhere else. I wandered aimlessly about the house, unable to rest for more than a short time. I would begin one task only to leave it unfinished and start another. Yet I had no real focus and no energy. Since no one talks much about these things, few understand this kind of torpor. People who left a message on my telephone asking me to ring back might just as well have asked me to run a marathon. It is not that I did not want to call, but I simply did not have the energy to do so. Asking me out would receive the same kind of negative response. Strange as it may seem, in these earlier days those who were most helpful were friends who did not go to the trouble of asking but simply told me what I was to do. 'We are coming over for lunch and bringing fish pie. All you need to do is open a bottle of wine!' At least it got me moving, but it was by tapping into the energy of friends, because I simply had none that I could generate for myself. At this time I depended a good deal on other people taking the initiative. Left to myself, I simply wanted to be at home alone. A friend, himself bereaved, told me that the time comes when you have to start to accept invitations, even though you really do not want to be bothered. I found that was true, but it was yet quite a way down the road.

I suppose that, on reflection, because so few people talk of the direct experience of grief, there was no ready visual language available to me. I became conscious of the paucity of language in the context of the pain of grief and at times how misleading that language can be. I tried hard to avoid saying that I had 'lost' my wife. Somehow that seemed to me to imply that I had mislaid her and if only I looked hard enough I would find her again. Undoubtedly, there is for some a serious component of searching in grief and a need to go back to where someone much loved has died, or where the person was last seen and known. It was not so for me but I do understand the need, especially if death has come suddenly and unexpectedly. But death, in this world, is death, and its finality here and now cannot be avoided. That is not to say I did not feel lost and all at sea. Certainly, I was lost within myself and struggling to understand what was going on inside. There is no accessible language in our society that enables people to say what they feel inside. There are no ready common images that can be used to convey these feelings. Since we do not easily talk of grief, our culture heightens that sense of dis-integration. This sense of dis-integration was precisely the feeling of being lost in a deserted, strange and alien place.

When H died, the life I had known died too. Nothing could take away the love we shared, but the life we had made together was now gone and with it much of what had given me my identity as husband, lover, companion and friend, forged over more than four decades. No one told me of the sense of dis-integration that comes with grief. If my world seemed to fall apart, and if a good deal of what held me together was now gone, then it is not so surprising that I felt at times that I was breaking up, becoming dis-integrated, inside. The familiar landscape of relationships, work, future plans, shared memory now appeared distinctly like a foreign land. Memory became decidedly odd. I would forget things more readily and my family talked of things I could not remember. Perhaps this is some kind of protection. Memory meant acute and distressing pain. Just as, in a physical sense, when a hand or leg has been injured it is for a time too painful to touch, so memory was just too raw to go near. In all this, when I believed that I was hanging on by my torn and bleeding fingernails, I came to recognize that I was hanging on to nothing. But somewhere deep inside I realized that the profound and mysterious reality I had embraced in 'faith' was hanging on to me.

I have no doubt that in all this, some must have believed that I had lost my faith. Frankly, you need energy to have a crisis of faith and I had no energy even for that. On the other hand, the assumptions that some people made I found very difficult. 'It must be such a comfort having your faith at times like this' was one I heard quite often, and as far as I am concerned it revealed a fundamental misunderstanding of the nature of 'faith'. For me there are many words to describe what it means to embrace 'faith', and among them I would want to see 'challenging', 'disturbing', 'provocative' – but 'comforting' is not one of them. Nor do I believe that any of the spiritual giants whom I admire so much would ever consider 'faith' to be some kind of comfort blanket when times get tough. Profound human questions and deep human emotions are no easier to avoid for the person who embraces 'faith' than for anyone else. From the beginning I wrestled with the big questions of meaning and purpose, though in all honesty, H never asked, 'Why me?' and I never asked, 'Why us?' What measure of faith was ours never prompted those kinds of self-centred questions. I do understand that this kind of question is very pressing for some people, as they struggle to find some meaning in what is happening to them. It was simply not so for us. In the end I had no energy to wrestle with big questions any longer, but that is very far from saying faith was abandoned. In some curious way faith became a more embracing reality in which I was simply content to be.

Then there are those who talk too glibly about the process of grief. To talk of 'process' at all seems to imply a beginning, a middle and an end. The impact and character of grief certainly changes with time, but I am not yet able to believe it will ever 'end'. Nor do I want it to end, for that would be to deny the fact that grief is the other side of love. In life love grows and deepens. I am not now sure what happens to that love in death. I wonder if it will change. Perhaps it will. As C. S. Lewis discovered: 'in grief nothing "stays put"'. The pain may one day not be quite so acute, and that in itself may help in the recovery of my memory. In that case, I can see that love and pain will always be together. As nothing stays put in grief, there is still the opportunity that love will continue to deepen.

One thing I have learned over the years is that there is no straightforward set of categories into which grief can be safely packaged, and the truth of that needs to be more widely acknowledged. Shortly after H died I went to see a long-standing friend with whom I knew it was safe to talk and even to shed tears. He greeted me at the door saying, 'There is no grief like your grief.' He did not mean that grief was worse for me than for anyone else. He did not mean that my grief was special when put alongside that of other people. But it was a kindly acknowledgement that my grief was unique to me and that anyone who claimed to know what was going on inside me simply did not have the faintest clue. It was one of the most perceptive insights anyone made in those early days. Yet from some others came the unspoken but real assumption that I would 'get over it' and life would return to normal, without their ever seeming to realize that for me there was no 'normal' any longer.

It is helpful when grief is acknowledged, but then what is needed is space and time for the important work inside that needs to be done. Part of that work is a reintegration of the self that is struggling to find a new identity in a radically changed world. No one ever told me that, and one consequence for me was a serious loss of confidence. Speaking in public literally gave me the shakes. I no longer trusted my judgement, and certainly not my pastoral judgement. I questioned whether I had the patience any more to listen to people who thought that the world revolved around them. I knew that there were those who believed that their 'problem' was so serious as to demand a great deal of my time. Serious to them, of course, but to my mind in the great scheme of things only marginally above trivial.

By contrast I found myself more deeply sensitive to those struggling in different contexts with their own reality of loss.

In particular I found myself connecting with those who were able to tell their inside story of grief. Some of the most vivid descriptions of grief I have found were written by women in the aftermath of divorce, even when their divorce was the result of their husband's betrayal or continual violence. Among the most heart-rending are accounts written by soldiers who have lost limbs when blown up by roadside bombs. In earlier times many would not have survived, but now they have the greatest challenge of facing full-on the kind of life they have lost while rebuilding what they have into the very different future that lies before them. The courage to come to the point where it is possible to use the pain of what is past to weave a potential new future is a significant element in the work of grief.

However, I am still trying to work out what that means when it comes to looking forward to a life that seems at times to be achingly empty. An essential part of the life that H and I shared was planning ahead for the things that we would do together. It now seems odd to try to plan things for myself alone. Maybe this is why decisions are difficult to make.

In recent decades a good deal of analysis has been done in trying to study the nature of grief. Such research has greatly enhanced our understanding, especially when people after several years are 'stuck' in their grief and can no longer function well. Sometimes there is an all too easy assumption that grief is depression, whereas depression can simply be one of several common characteristics of grief. I discovered that there are many labels that can be attached to grief. But none of them really helped me to have a conversation with myself. I simply could not find the imagery to do justice to what I was feeling inside without somehow diminishing it.

In fact, past ages have used a whole raft of words to try to describe the disposition of the human spirit. None of these is synonymous with grief and none of them specifically refers to it, but the inner feelings they describe share certain characteristics. *Accidie* was widely used in the Middle Ages and revived in the Romanticism of the nineteenth century. Thomas Aquinas called it a 'torpor of the spirit', and Chaucer in 'The Parson's Tale' wrote that 'accidie maketh a man, heavy, thoughtful and wrawe' and it 'forsloweth and forsluggeth a man whenever he attempts to act'. Accidie was closely associated with the sin of sloth preventing a person doing any good, but its root lies in the Greek word *akedos*, which means 'without care', a sort of empty indifference. It is used of those in defeat on the battlefield who cannot summon the energy even to bury their dead.

Melancholy, literally 'black bile', was well known to the Greeks. Melancholy was not limited to a mental disposition but was believed to present with physical symptoms including lack of attention, weakness of limbs, a debility of focus and a disturbed sleepiness. *Tristitia* is another term widely used in the past to denote a deep sadness. William Byrd's motet '*Tristitia et anxietas*' captures something of its essence: 'Sadness and anxiety have overtaken my inmost being. My heart is made sorrowful in mourning; my eyes are become dim.' Interestingly, in Islam a similar condition is widely acknowledged, especially by Sufis, who use the term *Huzun* to describe the 'sighs of the sorrowful heart'.

For my part, I soon realized that I simply did not know how to talk to myself about what I was feeling, let alone make sense to anyone else. It may be that we have been so seduced by definition that we have robbed people of a voice and a language with which to convey, however haltingly, what they feel inside. More and more I found myself going to poetry to find an elusive language I might use. In fact I was looking for some picture language that would bear the weight of what I felt. Curiously, it was two paintings that at one point helped me to understand something of myself.

Just over a year after H died I went to the United States to do a little work in a large Episcopal church. It was, on my part, a test of confidence to see whether I could still function with some of my former skills. It was not an easy time, but with some help I was able to confront a few demons and get through some challenging situations.

Coming back from the United States I knew that something had shifted inside me, but I could not find the words to describe it. When I returned home I was invited to a local art gallery where an up-and-coming artist was exhibiting his work. Two pictures immediately caught my eye and at first I thought they were identical. The pictures were of a seascape. The first, called *Steel Sky*, was of cold, grey brooding clouds over a dark and threatening sea. I recognized in that picture some of what I had felt inside. A brooding darkness, shut in, yet being tossed on a cold and threatening sea that at any moment might utterly overwhelm me. Then, when I looked closely at the second picture, it was undeniably the same scene but the hues were different. Subtle but fundamental changes of tone gave it a different feel altogether. The title of the second picture was *Breaking Through*. Here in these pictures the scene was just the same. The constituent parts of the pictures on the face of it were identical, but subtle changes of tone made me sense a change without anything important being lost. The pictures represented something that had shifted in me, but a shift I could not readily find words to explain. I returned to the gallery the next day with the intention of buying the pictures. They had already been sold.

Since I was struggling so much to find language and imagery to describe what was going on inside me, it is no surprise that music came to play an important role in my conversation with myself. I could recognize in some music what I felt inside even when words failed. The lament in particular was able to carry profound emotion with that deep sense of yearning yet with an inner strength that in the end was a kind of balm. There can be something of a lament in the lullaby. Think of Johannes Brahms' 'Lullaby'. The lament is a phenomenon across cultures, from the beginning of a jazz funeral in New Orleans to the haunting lament of the Scottish bagpipes. Just think of

George Gershwin's 'Summertime' or Cole Porter's 'Every Time We Say Goodbye'. Lament has given us the music of remembrance. Here, in a place way beyond words, a deep place I cannot fathom, I found that pain and anguish, life and loss could be held together without denial or diminution.

Strangely, I recognized that place as a place of authentic prayer. 'In prayer it is better to have a heart without words than words without a heart,' wrote John Bunyan, and T. S. Eliot recognized that prayer is more than an order of words or the conscious occupation of the praying mind. There is a kind of liberation when words no longer get in the way. This was not a place of 'asking' or 'raging', or indeed of any active process at all. It was simply a place 'to be'!

Yet still I had not found a voice to talk to myself in a way that made some kind of sense of what I felt was going on inside me. Was I grieving? Well yes, of course, but that did not of itself give me a voice to describe all I felt. Was I depressed? Well, in one sense, because I was in a dark place I suppose that might have been said, but it was not enough and I would not have readily described myself as being depressed.

Gradually I came to see that there was a connection of images all the time but I had failed to recognize them. Whenever I struggled to describe what was going on inside I had, unconsciously, found myself using words to do with water and often to do with the sea. I had found myself lost and 'all at sea'. I was at a low ebb and tossed about by waves of grief. Maybe, at last, I was beginning to tune in to an ancient wisdom that does not try to define or label experience but is more imaginative in giving voice to describe it. Common images and symbols are essential to the work of interpretation. It is how I talk to myself and how I communicate feelings to other people.

In the ancient world the sea was always an image that could be used of chaos and confusion. After all, it was a common experience that in a moment the gentle tranquillity of sailing might be overwhelmed by the storm of wind and waves. You get a sense of that at the beginning of the Bible in the story of Creation. The Spirit of God moves over the waters and the waters below are separated from the waters above. Even here there is the distinct impression that the waters are only kept apart by the God who gives life, and that without that the waters of chaos will come flooding back. Such imagery is there in the story of Noah and the Ark. It is there again in the affirmation of love in the poetry of the Song of Solomon:

> Love is strong as death,
> passion fierce as the grave . . .
> Many waters cannot quench love,
> neither can floods drown it.
>
> (Song of Solomon 8.6–7)

Then there is the final, profound vision at the end of the Bible:

> I saw a new heaven and a new earth; for the first heaven and the first earth had passed away, and the sea was no more.
>
> (Revelation 21.1)

So when Psalm 69 gives voice to human anguish, crying out:

> Save me, O God: for the waters are come in, even unto my soul.
>
> (Psalm 69.1, BCP)

. . . that is exactly what I felt inside. The waters had come into my soul. I had lost all buoyancy and it was as if no amount of silent screaming could prevent my being overcome by waves of uncontrollable anguish. I was swamped by an immense heaviness where no one could reach me. More than that, I had no desire for anyone to reach me. Those who have come close to drowning tell of a certain lethargy, even resignation, that takes over after all the struggle and striving has been expended. This is what I felt and this was all-encompassing of body, mind and spirit. This was simply the totality of my being, for the waters had entered my soul.

Imagination is the seedbed of human sympathy. It is only through imagination that I can connect with another human being in his or her distress when I have no direct experience of what that person is going through. Fundamental to imagination is a fluency with images that we have in common and symbols with potential to stimulate human empathy and compassion. The great advances that have been made in the analysis of mental states and the definitions of mental stress cannot be denied, but more basic to human understanding is the capacity to give voice to what is going on inside, not just in terms of psychology but in pictures and images that others will recognize. I did not have the pictures to convey what I felt. No images readily came to mind, and in that state my imagination had been numbed, along with much else. All this made me more isolated and alone in my dark and, at times, frighteningly dissonant world.

Even after two years I am not sure where I am in this still strange landscape. I am grateful for those who have been with me and stayed by me. It would have been all too easy for them to walk away.

'Grief', wrote C. S. Lewis, 'is like a long valley, a winding valley where any bend may reveal a totally new landscape.' Sometimes there is a feeling of familiarity, but it is never quite the same as what has gone before. At times I still struggle to understand what has gone on – and is still going on – inside me. However, I am now able to talk to myself in a way that makes sense to me. Beyond that lies a mystery that can never be fully fathomed, since it is the treasure of life that once was shared and no longer is. Grief continues to be an expression of love that, though it will change, I cannot believe will ever end. It seems there is something of infinite importance in the treasure of love that will for ever remain a mystery, just beyond my grasp. But then, as C. S. Lewis concluded: 'The best is perhaps what we understand least.'

2

New life I never wanted

JENNIFER REPLOGLE

On Friday, 22 October 2010, I watched as flames consumed Immanuel Chapel at Virginia Theological Seminary (VTS), where I was completing a year of Anglican studies prior to my ordination. I had never seen such uncontrolled fire. It ravenously consumed every timber and went unquenched by seemingly infinite amounts of water. When I ceased looking at the flames, and even after I closed my eyes that night, the fire remained present through the unavoidable smell of smoke. Etched into my mind as the sight of that fire is, the smell remains the most powerful memory of that day and the days to follow.

Five days later, on Tuesday, 26 October 2010, my dad left home in Louisiana on a trip to South Dakota. An hour into his journey, he was stopped behind a lorry and in front of a pickup truck. Another lorry, still travelling at high speed, ploughed into the pickup behind – pushing Dad's vehicle under the lorry in front of him. The impact caused Dad's car to explode, and the ravenous appetite of flames consumed his life, and life for my mom, sister and me as we knew it.

I learned the news that evening when I received my mom's life-changing call. The next 72 hours brought the whirlwind of a flight home, a wake and a beautiful funeral amid the love and presence of family and friends, followed by their gradual departures. Almost exactly a week to the hour after I stood watching one ravenous fire, my family opened the few items

18

partially spared by the fire that consumed Dad's life. We opened his hunting toolbox; the exterior was melted but it contained a few of his many gadgets. Half of his suitcase was covered in a strange fur produced by singed polyester. The flames had only spared the last inches of his suitcase in the very rear of the car, leaving some clothes – mostly burned and soaking wet, but still packed in his meticulously organized, tidy way. Somewhere in the wreckage my cousin found Dad's Bible – a small, travel-sized volume with a burned front cover.

What was so frighteningly familiar was the smell. It radiated from those few relics of my dad's last hours. I had smelled it so recently in Virginia as I witnessed the voracious appetite of the element that leaves such a smell in its wake. The smell forced a connection that my mind and heart were unable to make – how someone so alive could be reduced to so little, as quickly as the rafters of the chapel.

All deaths are difficult, but the difficulty of each manifests in forms as unique as the life that was ended and the lives that are changed. Because Dad was so alive until he was not, I do not know what it is like to watch a loved one suffer over a long period; I have no idea what I would do with an opportunity to say goodbye. Yet, after Dad died, I was grateful that I had been given an opportunity to say much of what I would have wanted him to know if I had known what was to come. Just six months before the accident, Dad retired from the company for which he had worked for 38 years. For the retirement party, family members and friends were asked to say what we had learned from him through his work; the statements were compiled for a surprise video. I wrote:

> In watching my dad work for this company throughout my whole life, I have been inspired by how he pours all of his energy into any work he undertakes while always being there for our family, and speaks up for what he believes is right while encouraging peace among people. Perhaps most of all, Dad

never meets a stranger because he approaches every person as someone who is worth talking to, hearing from, and knowing. I am grateful to have watched my dad live consistently through so many situations, and I love him.

Not only was it an opportunity to tell him this, but in the process of reflecting and writing, I realized it for the first time. Dad's tendency to talk to everyone about anything sometimes drove me crazy and, especially in my younger years, embarrassed me. With a few years of maturity and some time to reflect, I realized what actually drove that impulse was an incredible part of who he was. This was validated in the days and weeks following his death in the constant chorus of people talking about how friendly and kind he was, and their astonishment at the breadth of his knowledge and ability to engage across spectra of people and subjects. Though I did not know how widely this was thought, I am so grateful that I did not wait till after he died to realize it and tell him.

Another coincidental opportunity that was a blessing in hindsight was that just two weeks before the accident, Dad wrote and presented his spiritual autobiography to a group at church. He began with his older brother, Buddy, who died of leukaemia before Dad was born. The years of struggle and the eventual loss of their first child rooted the faith of Dad's parents, which surrounded him in his first home. Reading this for the first time, as I was reeling in my own unfathomable loss, I was fascinated that in Dad's simply written account of his own life, he communicated how his very soul was connected to a brother he never knew. His parents' work to create a loving home for all of their children meant making it through each day of grief, which was the continuation of love for a son whose presence had become absence far too soon.

Three weeks after Dad's death, I met with a friend, priest and now colleague, the Revd Sarah Kinney Gaventa. She put into words the truth I encountered in Dad's autobiography.

Sarah told me to remember that my relationship with Dad had changed incredibly, but that it was not over. When she said it, I could not imagine it through the still-thickening wall of numbness and shock. Simultaneously, I knew deeply it was true and, in retrospect, it has helped me understand much of this journey.

Perhaps it is in the radical change of relationship in death that we become most aware of how profoundly others are part of who we are. When we lose someone close to us, we know that we have lost a part of ourselves. Before I could fathom intellectually or emotionally that Dad was gone, my patterns of sleeping, eating, talking and thinking changed – marking profound changes in body, soul and self. I have long found hope in a faith that says that we are all part of each other and are who we are because of each other. When a relationship is altered in that most drastic way, we know we are changed by that altered relationship and we learn that living in communion is the essence of our created nature. I love those beautiful words written by John Donne nearly 500 years ago, 'No man is an island,' but I do not think I really knew the truth of intertwined humanity until I experienced the painful reality of my life washing away with Dad's.

Many of the details leading up to that moment when Dad was caught in the flames and of the hours that passed will never be known. Mom grew alarmed at Dad's lack of response to her calls, and by evening our house was teeming with friends who joined the search effort. In uncertain moments like these, our overactive imaginations instinctively create possibilities we all fear. Yet as the minutes ticked by without news of Dad, and those possibilities grew into probabilities, imagination became the faculty to which all turned in hope of conceiving any explanation other than the dreaded tragedy.

Around 8 p.m. a highway patrol car parked in front of our house. As Mom walked up, the officer slammed his computer shut. She enquired about Dad; he replied that he knew nothing and was waiting for his supervisor to arrive. She pleaded with him to tell her what he knew, and he refused. He remained there for over 45 minutes. He would have been out of sight if he had parked 100 yards away, but instead my mom, my sister and everyone in the house was tortured by an unofficial confirmation that the worst was true. At the same time they were denied an explanation, and with it a recognition of the depth of their loss, which would affirm the dignity of the husband, the dad, the friend whose absence was already real but which they were unable to mourn until that explanation was forthcoming.

Finally, a knock on the door signalled the presence of two highway patrolmen. Mom's usual Southern hospitable, polite nature was bypassed as she opened the door demanding, 'Where is my husband?' The senior officer insisted that they came in and sat down. Sitting in my father's chair, he minced no words: 'There was an accident. There was a fatality. It was your husband.'

When Mom called me, I was enjoying a glass of wine on the patio at VTS with my friends, Betsy, Jonathan and Chase. She said she was glad I was not alone because she had the worst news imaginable. My heart dropped into my stomach – I did not know how it happened, but I immediately knew what that meant. She said Dad had been in a car accident. 'Jenny, he didn't make it.'

It's strange how your mind can be unbelievably still, and spinning with thoughts at the same time. I knew I heard the words, and I knew what they meant, but there is no word I can think of besides 'surreal' to describe what began then. I stood up because I couldn't sit, but then it seemed that my knees had forgotten how to function. While I was talking to Mom, my cousin Brian arrived. He lived nearby and Mom had the foresight to call him so that I would not be alone. I ran to him and he held me. With my head against his chest, I felt him begin to cry, and I was able to let the first tears fall.

The only times that I remember crying in those days were like that – when I was held by someone else who was crying.

Alone, I had few tears. Perhaps my body had forgotten what to do so much that it took another person to guide me. I remember being told that it was OK to cry, as if I was holding it in. Quite the contrary – I had nothing to let out. Crying seemed so normal, so natural – and I did not feel normal or natural. I was not afraid to show emotion; no expression of emotion previously experienced seemed adequate. Tears were not enough.

A vigil was kept in my room that night by friends who would carry me through the next several months. I remember little of what was said but I will never forget their presence. I most remember Betsy, who held my hand and put her arm around me, always touching me somehow. We were not very close at this point, and I am slow to become affectionate with others, so this was entirely her instinctive initiative. I just remember being glad.

I never would have known to ask for this, but I needed it. My mind and body had already begun to create the numbness that would envelop me. It is an incredible instinct that protects us, but in cutting off connection to that which we cannot yet handle, it untethers us from everything. I'm convinced that it takes someone else holding on to keep us tethered. Betsy held on. Her hands felt like they were literally keeping me grounded, letting me know that I was still there and that I was not there alone.

Perhaps Betsy's hands are the physical sign of the grace of friendship that carried me. So many people offered to do anything I needed or asked how they could help, but I did not know what I needed or wanted. I did not know 'how to grieve' and had no answer for their offers. Those who carried me were those who held on to me when I could not reach out for them.

Because we are created for communion, when one relationship is altered in this most drastic way, all others are affected. In these moments, the relationships that make us who we are shift, making all of life seem bizarre and unfamiliar. The time of greatest exhaustion and weakness demanded the energy to begin life all over again, to learn to live a new life I desperately did not want. From that place, I found it impossible to reach out or even respond, and it is only because of the hands of friends who held on to me that we maintained any relationship. I survived because of those who continued to call, show up, invite and insist, and just do things that I no longer had the energy to even desire. I was grateful, but writing to thank someone became impossible: writing, which had been my best way of expression, became impossible overnight, as I could muster so few words that it seemed they would cheapen the presence and love offered, the power of which was keeping me alive.

Later that night I knew I should call some friends, but when I did I struggled to explain the reason I had called. Saying the words seemed to make it more real, and I was desperately hoping this was a bad dream. Friends wake you up from a nightmare; friends correct you when you say something erroneous. As I contacted different people from various areas of my life, rather than pulling me out, they entered into the nightmare with me. Being in the nightmare with me is what I needed and am now grateful for, but then I just wanted the nightmare not to be true. As each of them heard the news and did not shake me awake to return me to the reality I wanted to be true, the nightmare became more real.

I flew home the following morning, feeling torn. I knew that I should want to be at home, want to be with family. But I did not. The desire to be with family during this time faded in comparison to how much I did not want this to be happening. Dad was not usually present in Virginia; I knew when I returned home, where his presence was a constant, that his absence would be overpoweringly real. I dreaded being with other people for whom life had stopped, so I dreaded being with my family. I dreaded being in our house knowing he never again would be, and so I dreaded going home. This was the first of many instances of being baffled by the question: 'Do you want to . . . ?' For many months to come, I screamed inside that of course I did not want to, because I did not want any of this to be happening.

Our house was busy by the time I arrived. Many family and friends were there, and would be for the next several days. It is another paradox that I have experienced repeatedly. I do not know what we would have done without their presence, but no matter how many people are present, there is one huge absence that is almost more tangible. Yet the only way that I have survived that absence is by knowing how deeply loved I am, which I have known through the presence of so many people in my life.

Around this time, I learned that the presence that would become the most powerful would arrive the next day. Jonathan and Betsy had decided that he, Jonathan, should come for the funeral. Following chapel that morning, the Dean of Students at VTS, Dr Amy Dyer, told him that the school would pay for his flight if he would go. Then she spoke a truth that would increasingly manifest in the months to come: 'We don't suffer alone. We suffer in community.'

My family made the initial preparations at the funeral home while I was travelling home, so I did not see the casket until we arrived Thursday evening for the visitation. This was the first tangible symbol of death I encountered. Before, it was just absence around the house, but now there was an object that was an unmistakable new presence, a sure sign of what was inside – and who was not.

It was certainly closed casket – we were relieved of the horrific task of identifying my dad's body because there was not enough left to recognize him. Nonetheless, the owner of the funeral home asked us to provide clothes to bury him in, because he said all bodies were sacred, regardless of condition. My sister was married just four months earlier, and Mom chose the clothes that he wore for that occasion. Our last family picture is from the wedding. Every time I look at it, I think that the suit that once held a man so alive is now buried with . . . with what? Certainly not Dad. I shudder to think what it holds; what it looked like then, before decay began its work. How can one so alive be reduced to ashes in the blink of an eye?

The funeral was Friday at Christ Church, Covington, an Episcopal parish where my parents had been members for less than a year. It was the definition of beauty in tragedy, a shimmer of light in the midst of darkness. During the visitation before the funeral, the Revd Anne Maxwell came in saying, 'Come with me. We're going to do priest things.' The casket was being carried into the church. She opened her prayer book, put her arm around me, and prayed to receive the body into the church.

Although I had seen the casket the evening before, it had been difficult to take it in because the visiting line began immediately after we arrived. Standing in the church with Anne, cracks of reality started creeping their way through my wall of numbness. It had by no means sunk in, but it was the beginning of grasping the awful truth. But in that moment I was held, with Anne's arm around me.

The funeral was a corporate, liturgical expression of that experience. In beautiful words and music, the work of people held us. As those cracks of reality started crawling in, they were accompanied by glimpses that it might be possible to face the tragedy. We sang good old hymns. The Revd Tom Blackmon preached a great sermon that was true to Dad. There were jokes – Dad had probably been introduced to his new collection of tools and started working to fix anything that needed it, starting with the pearly gates.

We shared communion, the most powerful part of the service. In these times, hope cannot be explained but it can sometimes be lived. We shared the bread and wine, knowing that the communion we share, that brings us all together here, is shared among us all, and that while death mightily changes our communion, it does not bring it to an end. Dad's physical presence among us was gone, and although I did not yet consciously understand it, I had already experienced profound changes in my own body. In these times, perhaps it is not surprising that the greatest way to express that the relationship still remains is consuming bread and wine in the hope that what we take into our bodies is still shared with those whom we can no longer see and touch.

Regardless of familiarity, each element of the service is for ever entwined with that day in my memory. Whenever I hear one of the hymns, I remember that day. It doesn't erase their beauty or negate the power of singing them in community, but they are for ever changed for me. I remember singing, and feeling that great communion present in music, knowing that I could somehow face this now, surrounded and embraced in that moment but aching for it never to end, unable to imagine returning alone to a normal life in which no day would ever be normal again.

While I had known the hymns my entire life, this was the first time I encountered the funeral liturgy that is a fundamental part of my work as a priest. Those words, those prayers, will always be attached to loss of my own. I cannot pray them without remembering feeling as if the core of my bones had been sucked out. I am sure many would disagree on whether or not this is good – my focus in other funerals will never completely be on the one for whom those words are being said at that moment. I feign no objectivity, but we all bring our own experiences to walking with others. These words will never be separate for me from my own grief, and this creates connection because it is the closest I can come to knowing the grief of those whom I accompany in their mourning.

After the funeral, we invited everyone to our house. In so many ways, the time was wonderful: the people gathered, the stories told, the laughter and love shared. I learned about parts of Dad's life I had not known; I was learning how other people knew him and thus coming to know him in a new way myself.

However, that new sweet knowledge was bitter because it could not be separated from losing the way I had known him.

Shortly afterwards I wrote,

> The stories of my dad have now joined the folklore of our family – stories of those of whom there will be no new stories to tell. There are many funny stories which still make me laugh so hard, but now the tears in my eyes are not tears of joy. The touching stories make me smile, but my heart breaks because no more will be touched by him. I cannot stop listening and telling them, because there is something healing in the repetition. But that does not change that each story is a reminder that there will be no more about him.

Later, Jonathan went with me to look at the luggage. I remember being unsure about asking him. He did not need to see it; I feared that I was being melodramatic or sensationalistic. But somehow I needed him to see it with me. With my family, I needed to be strong – not that I was the strong one, but we all had to be strong for each other. I needed someone else to see the darkness who was not in it.

All deaths are difficult, but the difficulty is always unique because the separation between us is a part of the relationship between us. As every relationship is the *sui generis* connection between two unique people, the journey of grief is no less of its own kind because it is the work of continuing that relationship after the most drastic change of all, death. No matter how many mourn a death together, we find ourselves alone in our grief. My mom, my sister and I grieved together, but our own special relationships with my dad made our grief equally special. The loneliness inside grief can be terrible and terrifying, yet it is sacred because it is the other side of love.

Yet it is possible to accompany another in this lonely, sacred space. Within my isolating disconnectedness, I found the most profound connections with those who walked in the darkness with me. Those who accompany another inside grief walk in a strange and special place. They need to face the darkness fully, yet it is important for the darkness not to be their own. Because they have chosen to be there, their presence forms a bridge to life in a world that has become foreign.

Jonathan stayed for a week. Months later, friends and family talked about how amazing he was – and it was true. He somehow knew how to be there any time we needed him, but gave us plenty of space when we did not. I know he helped with various logistics, but what I remember is that he was there. I was screaming inside when family left after the funeral, because I did not know how I would face that house, soon to be empty except for Mom and me. It did not seem less empty, but having Jonathan there with me helped.

The last night Jonathan was there was the night that Dad should have returned home from South Dakota. The previous week's events were traumatic, but the permanence of his absence was slightly masked because until then he was supposed to be on a trip. That day a new dimension of the reality that he was not coming home set in.

Jonathan made dinner that night while Mom and I watched. Jonathan is one of those people who makes cooking art, both in the final result and in the process of creation. Watching him cook was therapeutic, partly because of the normality of preparing daily food and partly because it was beautiful. Sometimes beauty is found in extraordinary places and normality means mundane rhythms, and sometimes they are intertwined. For a soul disconnected in grief, there is incredible power in beauty and normality because there is a mystery in them that is recognized in a time when little else is. A few days later, Mom described it best when she spoke of our meal together: 'It was communion.'

Two weeks after the accident, I returned to VTS just in time for our weekly chapel service, and I went longing for the normality of prayer rhythms and hoping for the beauty that carried me during the funeral. Instead, I remember staring at the words of a hymn that began, 'Thy terrors now can no longer, death, appal us'. Really? I understood theologically what it meant, but it was asinine nonetheless.

A few weeks later, in the final chapel service of the semester, we sang a hymn that seemed a direct reply to the confusion brought on by that previous one. In the second verse of 'There's a wideness in God's mercy', we sang, 'There is no place where earth's sorrows are more felt than up in heaven.' I find far more hope in a heavenly throng that, having seen the beauty of fellowship available for us, laments all the more the realities we continue to face, rather than claiming that they do not appal us.

Death holds terror. Perhaps not all deaths are equally terrifying in their details, but death is terrifying. The circumstances of Dad's death are full of terror, and many are far worse. I have a hole in me because my dad is gone, and that hole tells me something about how I was created – that we are part of each other. Any attempt to soften the terror, quell how appalling death can be, simultaneously suppresses our ability to imagine the immense love of God for us and tears at the love between us and those we have lost, because grief is the continuation of that love.

When I returned to VTS I was hungry for normality, though I knew that nothing would make me feel normal. I hoped that studying, reading and writing – those things that I knew how to do, that I was good at, that I was accustomed to because they had consumed the several previous years – would provide something familiar in a world that was so unfamiliar. However, the world felt different because I was different, rendering the most familiar tasks most difficult.

I had always loved losing myself in thought, and felt most alive connecting and creating from the ideas spinning around in my mind. Suddenly I could not grasp anything. My mind was void of singular thoughts, so connecting disparate ones was certainly impossible. I read sentences over and over, knowing they conveyed something relatively simple but finding it incomprehensible. Previously, writing flowed easily, but in just a fortnight I was left struggling to formulate a few sentences in hours of effort. Earlier that year during exams at Princeton, I wrote over 100 pages in less than two weeks. In December, I was proud when I finally completed a mediocre three-page essay after six weeks of effort.

I was most frightened by my inability to remember anything. My memory was one of my most reliable strengths; suddenly, I could not remember simple details of conversations. I usually had a hazy recollection that a conversation had occurred and possibly of the subject discussed. The frustrating practical implications faded in comparison to the fear inherent in having too much memory to be comfortably oblivious and just enough to be aware that the workings of my own mind were unfamiliar and unknown. The loss of my dad ruptured my knowledge of my world and myself in a way that did not simply feel like fear. Inside grief, the disconnection reached the depth of rendering even my own self a stranger, and fear grasped me in that place where I no longer knew how to live and move and have my being. The real terror was that I did not know if I ever again would.

I have theoretically believed that we are whole creatures, not separated body, mind and soul, and that we are all connected more deeply than we recognize in our individual world. But in death, I have come to know these things are true. In addition to my mind, my body changed physically before I cognitively grasped the idea that my dad was dead. Patterns of sleeping and eating were altered. Initially I slept a lot, but after two months, sleep became a struggle. Regardless of sleep, I was always tired; there was always an incredible exhaustion that seemed to be in my bones and heart. The fatigue made my usual exercise difficult, decreasing an already suppressed appetite, and that compounding cycle changed my body before my mind had even begun to understand what had happened.

Even as my body slowly drifted back towards normal patterns of sleeping and eating, I knew the depth of the change through the way anniversaries seemed to be written into my body, a phenomenon the likes of which I had never experienced. On the 26th of each month I felt a physical exhaustion, accompanied by an emotional emptiness that exacerbated the exhaustion. The knowledge of this loss was manifested in January, when I mistakenly thought the 26th was the 25th. This happened in July as well. Both times I felt terrible and looked for another explanation for the severe exhaustion. When I realized the correct date though I had not cognitively known it, I was amazed by the effect of this loss within my body.

Grief is a strange journey. Different days can be quite similar and somehow not feel familiar. Throughout the year after Dad's death, the terrain involved small hills and deep valleys, but on the horizon there was a slow, gradual lifting of the cloud. However, in October, as the first anniversary drew near, I began to think I was depressed because of the growing exhaustion and regularity of tears. After months of a mostly uphill journey, I did not associate this with grief but rather looked to the stress of a new job or anything else that could possibly be blamed.

I woke up on the morning of 26 October and felt as if that weight had lifted, or at least shifted significantly. I was certainly sad, but I no longer felt the exhaustion of carrying several hundred extra pounds. There was still a profound absence in my world, but I knew it was a world that contained hope.

Eighteen months into this journey, I had another span of difficult weeks that I could not understand. The feelings were similar to October, but I assumed that part of the journey had been unique to the first anniversary. Engrossed in Lent and Holy Week planning, thinking in liturgical days rather than dates, I failed to realize until only a few days beforehand that Holy Saturday was Dad's birthday. When I awoke on 7 April, the weight had once again shifted. I was sad. Sometimes there were tears right behind my eyes, but they were different tears than were shed in previous days. These were purely tears that were sad that Dad was not celebrating another year of life, tears that wished I could call and wish him happy birthday, rather than the tears of frustration and futility that had threatened the previous weeks.

With each difficult moment, I learned to anticipate similar ones. That anticipation did not prevent those difficult times, but made them far more bearable. However, there were unexpected moments when it felt as though the rug had been pulled from under my feet. I clearly remember the worst one of those times. Having been ordained in June, I was hired as a curate and returned to Princeton, where I had completed my Master of Divinity. Only weeks after I began my work, one colleague was on maternity leave and another was on vacation, so I was the only clergy available to make visits to the local hospital.

I completely forgot that I had been to that hospital the previous summer, after catching a virus while my parents were visiting. Dad spent the day with me in the emergency room; even when I encouraged him to go eat, he would not leave my side. That was only days before he returned home, which was the last time I saw him. As I approached the hospital focused on visiting a parishioner, a tidal wave of memory swept over me. Everywhere I looked, I could only see a place I had been with Dad. In moments like those, presence and absence seem impossible to differentiate because they are both so palpable. All I was aware of was how much his presence was part of who I was and how terribly I missed him, making his absence tangibly present.

I tried to hold in tears momentarily, but this battle I could not win. Sitting in the parking lot, I broke down and sobbed. I considered calling someone, but I could not. It was not a lack of knowing there were willing and able people in my life available for me in these moments. The problem was I lacked the ability to choose someone to call and could not formulate words to explain what was happening, because I did not know what was happening. The only reason I had not melted into a puddle on the ground was because I was held between the seat and the steering wheel; I felt as if the ground itself had been pulled from beneath me. Those moments are terrible enough, but the real terror is that the enveloping helplessness whispers that it will certainly return, that no moment again will ever be free of the threat of such a sudden arrival.

The mystery inside grief is that within my numbing, frightening and isolating disconnectedness, the deepest human connections I've known were born. Because every grief is unique, it can only be fully known by the one who is in it, and thus it is a time of most intense disconnectedness. But on this lonely path, those who are able to walk alongside us and hold a hand become the light and life that carry us on that road of darkness and death.

Those who are able to enter that sacred ground are rare. Although most people mean well and are trying to help, often words convey that they cannot enter that place because they are trying to make better a situation where there are genuinely no words. 'He's in a better place.' 'At least you know you will see him again.' 'Your faith is strong, so you'll be OK.' Of all the things people said, one sentiment represented the most awful, unbearable idea inside grief: 'Well, we know it wasn't an accident; it's all part of God's plan.'

God planned this? I saw pictures of Dad's car after the accident. I saw the few things salvaged from the car. And I never saw his body again because he was burned beyond recognition. *What* God planned this? After years of studying theology, an articulate response to this was suppressed by sheer hurt and anger. Shortly afterwards, I read something by Richard Rohr that best expressed what I could not at the time:

> What we need to do is recognize what is, in fact, darkness and then learn to live in creative and courageous relationship to it. In other words, don't name darkness light. Don't name darkness good, which is the seduction that has happened to many

of our people . . . The most common way to release our inner
tension is to cease calling darkness darkness and to pretend it
is passable light.   (Rohr, 2008, p. 23)

Perhaps for some people, believing that God mechanically
controls and plans everything makes the world seem more
safe, more good, maybe more just. I cannot believe this, but
sometimes I think that if it works for them, it is OK. But do
not tell me that my dad's tragic, premature death is not dark.
And, please, do not try to make that explosion into anything
that remotely can pass as light.

Because I have now seen grief from the inside, I believe we call
the darkness a passable light from the outside because we are afraid
of it. Sometimes we can afford the luxury of avoiding the darkness when it surrounds someone else, but truly facing another's
grief forces us to face realities that we would rather avoid: our
lives and the lives of those we love are always a split second
from being drastically altered; all we do to control our life can
be trumped in a moment by a tragic decision, diagnosis or death.

From inside, it hurts when someone says that darkness is
not so dark, because it attempts to diminish the pain of grief
and in so doing strikes at the love from which that grief is
born. From inside, I knew what was darkness, and not only did
I not want it to be diminished, my stripped soul had no desire
for that parade of imitations that I knew were not real in comparison to the flickers of a Light that I was beginning to see.
From inside, I have come to believe that the greatest tragedy is
that when we shield ourselves from that darkness, we also shade
ourselves from the Light.

I find hope in John's beautiful telling of the Incarnation:
'What has come into being in him was life, and the life was
the light of all people. The light shines in the darkness, and the
darkness did not overcome it' (John 1.3–5). Believing in the
Light does not mean that the darkness ceases to exist. No,
the Light comes into the darkness and is not overcome by it.

Real hope can only be conceived in the darkness, when we leave a place for it. Leaving a place requires waiting, sitting, giving time for our eyes to adjust to the darkness, and that is the work of grief. Before his death, I could see or at least hear my dad; I did not have to hope that he was alive. For the first few weeks after the accident, I was so numb. Hope was that they had the wrong person, that Dad was not in that car and was still alive somewhere. Hope was that he would call soon. But that was not real hope. It was wishing – hanging on to a reality that no longer is. Only in the pain of knowing he is gone can true hope be born. Only in missing him, in walking with that hole in my heart rather than trying desperately to fill it, will there ever be room for a new thing to be done.

Hope looks forward to something new, but inside grief the new is intertwined with the pain of loss. For me, the journey of grief has been learning to live a new life that I never wanted. I can choose to hang on to a futile hope that the old life will return, but that is not real life. If I want to live, I must live with the emptiness that came in and around me.

In the emptiness, hope has been born. In this new life that I never wanted there have been moments of grace in the love that has surrounded me and the hands that have carried me. In this darkness, I have glimpsed God because here I have been overwhelmed by an awareness of how deeply loved I am. Light has come from people who have ventured into the darkness with me. They have been the light, and that light is powerful. That light is beautiful.

In the darkness of death, that light is Life.

References

Rohr, Richard (2008), *Preparing for Christmas with Richard Rohr: Daily Meditations for Advent*, Cincinnati, OH: St Anthony Messenger Press.

3

Death of a child

———•◆•———

MARY SLEVIN

The nightmare started on Easter Saturday, 14 April 1990, at 4 p.m., and to some extent it continues to this day. Before that it had been a normal Saturday. Kevin, my 20-year-old son, had been over to collect my mother – his beloved Nan – who was to stay with us for the weekend. About 2 p.m. he left the house calling, 'See you later, Mum.' He had arranged with his friend James to go shopping for a shirt to wear to a party.

I answered the phone to another of Kevin's friends, Simon, who had been driving along a fairly notorious local road when he came across the crash site. He recognized the car and stayed while the emergency services attended. Kevin had been travelling towards home with James as a passenger. They were taken by separate ambulances to the local district hospital. Simon said that while he had been told that James was being admitted, he was given no news about Kevin.

Kevin's father had died suddenly from a heart attack on Christmas night 20 years before, when Kevin was four months old and his brother Michael two years ten months. Life for me as a single parent and a working mother was a constant battle to survive, caring for the children, earning enough money to keep us afloat, and trying to provide them with the love, stability and support to enable them to develop into rounded adults. Now was the time I was just about breathing out. I had two young men to be very proud of.

My first response to the phone call was one of irritation, and this has been a huge cause of guilt for some years. I selfishly worried about how I could manage to care for him if, for instance, he had a limb or limbs in plaster or had to stay in hospital. I was working full time. Michael and I decided to drive to the hospital in separate cars, as he was planning to go straight out afterwards.

As I was driving along I speculated about the extent of Kevin's injuries. Supposing he had a head injury? Supposing he was left with permanent brain damage? I can still mark the spot along the road where the possibility that he might be dead suddenly hit me. The tears came and I started screaming inside. The thought was too terrible to absorb – life could not be that cruel, could it? But of course it could. Ever since my husband had died I had been afraid that IT was not over, whatever IT was. Now IT concerned the death of one of my sons.

Michael and I arrived at A&E simultaneously. We were both terrified. As we reached reception my worst fears were realized. No one said anything, but a nurse showed me into the 'family room' and pulled the curtain across the opening. I asked to see him. I needed to be with him. He was my son. I had given birth to him. Who else should be with him?

The trained nurse who ushered us in was about my age but she couldn't engage eye contact. Her only need seemed to be to get us out of the way. I knew from her demeanour that he was dead. To get out of the room she said she would make us a cup of tea. This would have been amusing if it hadn't been so tragic for us – I never drink tea and Michael rarely does. When the nurse reappeared some time later with the tea, I asked her again what was happening. Her reply was that the doctor would be along to speak to us. This doctor never materialized. Instead it was a very kind, gentle police officer who confirmed my worst fears. I am still angry that at a time when all I wanted was the truth, my own profession was so wanting in compassion it failed me. I know that nursing staff are not supposed to tell relatives about a death, but as Kevin's body was taken straight to the mortuary from the ambulance there was little doubt that he was dead. I was so worried about Michael, yet so distressed I found it hard to offer him any comfort; there was none to be had. I felt like there was such a heavy weight on my chest I would not be able to draw my next breath. This sensation became familiar to me in the weeks ahead. I truly felt that my heart would break.

I was then asked if I would be willing to identify Kevin's body. Of course – who else should? Michael wanted to accompany me. After a very long wait while the body was prepared, a little cortège – Michael and I and two policemen – set off down a long corridor in the basement, past all the changing rooms, the kitchens, the laundry – such a mundane environment, with people chatting and laughing at the end of their shift. I don't know how I managed to put one foot in front of another. I just wanted to scream and scream and beat the walls. But instead I learned again the lesson that everyone who is bereaved has to learn sooner or later. No matter how devastated they feel, the world around them still goes on; family, friends and acquaintances, however sympathetic and understanding, will sooner or later need to return to their everyday lives. The huge task for the bereaved is to try to make sense of this new world they now inhabit and, at some stage, rejoin it.

We reached the mortuary viewing room. The draped trolley was in the middle of the softly lit room. As a nurse I have seen and touched many corpses, but I was unprepared for how cold he was. As I felt his familiar face I could feel his broken jaw. I was aware that Michael was crying. It hit me that this was the first dead body he had seen, and it was the body of his much loved brother.

Somehow we made it back to the curtained alcove that served as the family room. A close friend of mine had joined us by then. I remember asking if Kevin could be anointed by a priest. This was very important to me. I also offered his organs for transplant, but of course it was too late. I know that in the case of unexpected death it can be an enormous comfort to relatives if the deceased person's organs are harvested. At least several other people can be offered a chance of life thanks to the senseless death of a loved one.

I know how important it is to be able to see the body; it helps the bereaved to accept the reality of the death. However, I know from other women that, following a traumatic death, the authorities, usually the police, consider that they should not view the body; that identification under such circumstances is a male task. This assumes that women are not emotionally strong enough to cope, and men are. I would dispute this.

The police drove us home. We arrived to a room full of people. Not long after we had set off for the hospital the police had called on my mother and delivered the terrible news. My mother had then started calling family and friends. The phone was constantly ringing and more people arrived, my brother and his wife reaching us after a nightmare journey from the Midlands.

I wandered around, picking things up and putting them down. I couldn't think. Intellectually, I knew Kevin was dead. I had seen and touched his corpse; there could be no doubt. But emotionally I couldn't accept it. No, no, no, it must be a mistake. Not the beautiful son that I had conceived and given birth to. I don't know what it would be like for a father, but for me as his mother I felt a physical connection to him. He was a part of me. I had nourished him with my milk and tried to ensure that he grew to be as healthy and fulfilled as possible. I had ensured he had all his vaccinations; I had been meticulous about maintaining dental appointments and shoe fittings; I had heard his reading and spellings, attended all his school open evenings, concerts, sports days and fundraising events, encouraged his sporting activities; I had acted as a taxi driver, ferrying both boys and their many friends around the area time and again. How could he be dead? Never again would I hear his voice or feel his touch or inhale the smell of him. I ached for comfort. All I wanted, then and now, was one of his bear hugs. He had always seemed very close to me as he had only had such a brief connection with his father. I had made a vow to myself after my husband's death that my children would always be my priority, and their well-being was the defining factor in any decisions I made about my life and theirs. I felt so sorry for them, when their father died, that they would never know, first hand, what a fine, loving man he was and how much he loved them.

My own father had died when I was ten and I had felt his absence very keenly for many years. I was the only child in my class who was without a parent, which in present-day society seems amazing. My brother, who was seven at the time, and I were not allowed to attend the funeral. I don't know who made that decision. I suspect that it was my father's mother and brother, as my mother was Irish and in her culture it is natural for everyone to attend burials and wakes. I was at the age where daughters and fathers are especially close. So it was with me. One of the most hurtful things people said then, and something that was constantly repeated, was that it was much worse for my brother than for me, simply because of his gender. This attitude made me so angry. I was also told by many people that I must be good and do all I could to help my mother, and not cry. As I was only ten, I am not sure how I could have achieved all this. My response was to keep all my feelings to myself – not to let anyone see how unhappy and confused I was. I became 'strong' but also an outsider, no longer belonging in the club of those who had two parents.

In the days ahead things became more confused. As well as all the phone calls, people kept arriving at the house. I had to give a statement to the police, who went out of their way to ease the process for me. The place where the accident happened was, and still is, a notorious black spot and it became apparent that the road surface had been greasy that evening. There was no evidence that Kevin had been speeding and he had no alcohol in his blood. His car had skidded sideways-on into a telegraph pole. At that time side impact bars were only fitted on very expensive cars, so the right side of his body had taken the full force of the crash. Despite medical assistance, he died in the car from multiple injuries and had to be cut out of it by the fire brigade. There are still visible gouges on the pole.

At some point on that Saturday evening a priest arrived. Although Father Michael was in his late thirties, he had only recently been ordained and had only just joined the parish, so I didn't know him. I later learned that he had never conducted a funeral; Kevin's was his first. To mix metaphors, it was a baptism of fire for him. Yet his inexperience was not obvious and in the months ahead I came to rely on him. He was especially supportive of Michael. Although Kevin was dead I was still the mother of Michael, but I found myself unable to offer him much help in his suffering. A few months later he spoke about how people would ask him how I was, but would rarely acknowledge his grief. He had become engaged the previous Christmas to his long-time girlfriend, Tracey, whom we all knew and loved. Along with his friends she provided invaluable support in those first months, and still does. A few days later Kevin's friend James, his passenger, arrived at the house following his discharge from hospital. I was so relieved to see him, if not fully recovered, at least mobile. I do not know how I could have borne it if he had died too, as Kevin would have been responsible. James had sustained a minor head injury and had no memory of the circumstances of the crash.

During the period between Kevin's death and funeral it became vital to me to collect any photos anyone had of him, to allow us to record his brief life. This became the most important part of my day. As he had died so young it felt very important to me to register that he had been alive. Then the hundreds of letters and cards started arriving. The ones that helped were those that simply said, 'I don't know what to say' and offered their love. There was nothing to be said. The ones that didn't help were those that said it was God's will. This was repeated by some members of the clergy in the months ahead. This enraged me. Where was this God of mercy? Had I not had enough taken from me: my father and then my husband? When would it be my turn to receive some of God's compassion?

Our parish church was packed for the funeral, with people standing outside. I had been able to work with the priest to select appropriate readings and hymns. It was important to be in control of something, as in everything else I felt helpless. Kevin had a thing about ants, and if he ever saw one in the house he had to catch and kill it. The one thing I could focus on during the funeral was the ant on the top of his coffin. I did eventually catch it. Seeing the coffin being lowered into his father's grave was excruciating. That space had been for me, not for my beautiful son. The natural order had been turned on its head: children should bury their parents, not vice versa. I will never forget hearing on the radio about coffin beetles, which invade the corpse from about three days after interment. The horror of the vision of my beautiful son's body being infested in this way stayed with me for many months.

After my father died I had been very lost and confused. After my husband died I was terrified – how on earth was I going to make a meaningful life for us? When Kevin died I felt hopeless. This blow was too cruel. That someone so vibrant with all his life before him should be dead . . . But life went on. As previously planned, Michael moved out six weeks later to live with his girlfriend. From a household bursting with two young men, their comings and goings, meals at all hours, a suddenly empty fridge, the mounds of laundry, music vibrating through the house, there was only emptiness and silence. I would go into Kevin's room and play his music loudly to try to connect with him. If I slept at night it was a help, but then I woke up. The novelist A. S. Byatt, whose son died aged ten in a road accident, spoke of forgetting to remember the reality of the death in the few split seconds after awakening, only to be hit with the truth yet again as she surfaced into consciousness.

It was hard even to get out of bed. Although I did not actively wish to end my life, I didn't want to keep on living. It was too hard to suffer all the pain. Those early days were filled with business and legal matters and many, many tears. I struggled on from hour to hour, from day to day. I dreaded meeting people whom I hadn't seen since his death. I learned quite quickly to deal with the platitudes, the ill-judged comments. I was encouraged to return to work, which I did after six weeks. Most days I just sat at my desk and wept. It is not a myth that some people will cross the street to avoid speaking to a grieving person. When I eventually managed to visit our HQ building, I was walking down a narrow corridor when someone I knew very well, and to whom I would previously have chatted, turned on her heel and disappeared. I was devastated, especially as I was working at a fairly senior level in the NHS. Even worse, my line manager never referred to my loss. To balance that, some work colleagues whom I barely knew went out of their way to contact me and offer support, especially those who had also suffered the loss of a child. They could accept and recognize my pain; we are in a terrible fellowship. Some months after Kevin's death there was a massive earthquake in the mountains of Iran. Television pictures showed a man in traditional dress carrying the shrouded body of his dead child. I instantly recognized the pain in his eyes. There was no need for words.

After about three months I just couldn't go on, and needed more time off work. My mother and brother were very supportive, as they had been since my husband had died, but of course they were grieving too. My mother had suffered for some years from cardiovascular disease. Seven months later she had a heart attack and died. Life was unreal. I was in the undertakers' paying for Kevin's headstone and arranging my mother's funeral. This was another blow for my son Michael. The boys had been very close to her; she had cared for them while I was at work. Then, another seven months further on, my brother's mother-in-law died. It felt as if we were smothered in death. I was lucky to have some really close friends who were amazing and were never deterred by the grief that hung around me. I think I fell back on the strategy I had used all my life since my father died. I tried to keep my feelings hidden, to avoid letting many people know how devastated I was and how vulnerable I felt. Each day I survived felt like a small victory. Four months after Kevin's death it would have been his twenty-first birthday. We invited friends and family to the house for a celebration of his life. Bereaved parents can often find themselves giving comfort to the young people who have been touched by the death. It is something that just doesn't happen to their generation and Kevin's friends found the finality unbelievable. So life went on. Friends supported us through the inquest and a verdict of accidental death was recorded; another step along the grief journey.

Sean O'Casey (1991) wrote following the death of his son of how the bereaved have to rejoin the rhythm of family life – baptisms, graduations, weddings, other funerals, engaging in conversations – but 'always the beloved one absent . . . always'.

In those first few months all I could do was fill my time with things that took no intellectual effort. I was exhausted – my head full of thoughts about Kevin, the events surrounding his death and the implications of his loss. I would sit for hours digging up clover from the lawn or doing a jigsaw. I also started reading voraciously any book I could get hold of where parents gave their account of the death of their child. I wanted to see if somehow someone, somewhere, had found the secret to surviving this catastrophe.

There are many models of recovery from grief, but each journey follows its own path. I subscribe to Tonkin's Model, illustrated by a ball placed inside a jar that it fills (Tonkin, 1996). Then the same ball is placed in a slightly larger jar, and so on and so on. The grief is represented by the ball and the jars of various sizes represent the world around us. The grief is there and always will be. It doesn't change size, but life slowly expands as we re-engage with it.

Michael Rosen, in *Carrying the Elephant*, written after the death of his son, describes seeing an illustration of a man bent double, carrying an elephant up a mountain, trying to walk while bent under the weight of it (Rosen, 2002). The terrain is rough with overhanging obstacles. But despite all the obstacles he hasn't fallen over, he is still carrying the elephant.

I gradually started taking small steps on my life's journey. Past my birthday, Christmas, my husband's anniversary, New Year, my wedding anniversary, Michael's birthday, Mother's Day and then Easter. Kevin had been dead for a whole year. I was invited to his friends' weddings, where I would be given the brides' bouquets to place on his grave – the nearest Kevin would ever get to a wedding. Then, further on, Michael's and Tracey's wedding, and eventually the births of my beautiful grandchildren.

Another friend whose son had also died in a car accident asked, 'What do I do with the love?' Well, what do we do? Do we continue to live or just have an existence? I firmly believe that the living must go on with life. There are those around you who need you to be a functioning human being. I slowly re-engaged with my professional life and gained promotion. I learned to laugh and to enjoy myself, even though there was always the guilt there – how could I laugh when my beloved son was dead?

Then I retired – in theory anyway. I decided to see if I would be accepted as a volunteer for Cruse Bereavement Care (see 'Further reading'). Following training I started working with bereaved people on a one-to-one basis and have continued to do so for 13 years. It is the policy of the organization that we do not disclose anything about our own personal bereavements, but hopefully the empathy that our experiences have given us can help those bereaved people who seek our support. This work is enormously rewarding and it is a privilege to be allowed to share people's sorrow with them. Bereaved people have a hard-won empathy to share with others in similar circumstances and, as I found, are willing to offer support when others fade away. Bereaved parents have looked into the chasm of grief and have survived.

Aristotle wrote: 'There is one loss from which a person can never recover, the death of a child.' But who is your child? Is it the miscarriage at 14 weeks, or the stillbirth or neonatal death? The toddler, the child, the teenager or young adult, or the middle-aged? They are all our children. The oldest person I worked with through Cruse was 94 years old. Her son had died from cancer aged 67. Her grief was acute, and was mixed with terror at the implications of her vulnerability at such an advanced age.

I hope that I have learned enough to avoid saying to someone in similar circumstances some of the more ridiculous or hurtful things that were said to me. Like the person who just a few weeks after the death of my husband commented, '**I know how you feel**, I had to have my dog put down some weeks ago.' No one knows how the bereaved person feels. Each person's grief is unique to that person. I may be able to support someone whose child has died in similar circumstances, but I do not know how that person feels. We know from research that over 70 per cent of relationships fall apart following the death of a child. Neither partner is able to support the other as they are drained dry and have nothing left to give. Even they don't know how the other really feels.

'**You'll get over it.**' No I won't, and I never will. What has happened is that my world has expanded, but my grief and sense of powerlessness have not. I can still be caught out by a memory or a sight or sound and dragged back to that terrible time. Kevin is still very much part of my internal life. I think about him every day and I am sure I will until I die. I wonder if he would now be married – have children of his own? Yet another loss for us.

'Closure'. This word has appeared in the last few years from across the Atlantic and is perhaps something we could send back. As a bereaved mother I don't know what it means. It is often uttered by those who have never suffered the death of someone close to them. I think it is a trite sentiment that people use to distance themselves from grief that they are unable to deal with. 'Well, you have now had the funeral/inquest/trial, so that is closure.' Except that, for those experiencing it, of course it isn't.

'**It's about time you started to get over it/get back to work/ go out socially. It will be good for you.**' The advice I offer is that in those early months and years, only you know what feels right to you; do not push yourself to meet other people's expectations. And avoid making irreversible decisions. You are not in a fit state to do so.

'**Time is a great healer.**' I spent time, following my husband's death, thinking that somehow I would wake up one day and life would be as it was before. Of course it never would be. I had to engage with the world as a new person. I shocked myself about five years afterwards by realizing that should my husband somehow come back, he would not recognize the person I had become. I had been forced by the circumstances of our lives to change.

'**You'll soon meet someone else/get married again.**' This was said to me for the first time at my husband's funeral. How crass was that? Well, although I did have some relationships, I have not married again. Not many available men beat a path to my door. I was very wary: not only would I be taking on a new partner, but also a stepfather for my children. As time went on I knew I could not take the risk. Anyway, my experience is that men leave me, and I didn't want any more pain.

'**You are lucky your husband has died, at least you know where you are, not like me.**' This has been said several times by people going through a divorce. Strangely enough I didn't feel that fortunate.

'Children are very resilient.' This implies that children do not feel grief, or that if they do it is transient and short term. There is now a large body of evidence that they do feel grief, and if they are unable to work through it, then they will carry adverse effects through into the rest of their lives. Children are often called the 'forgotten grievers', on the periphery of what is happening in the adult world. But children listen and look – not much gets past them. They are entitled to the truth, and to opportunities to express it. Someone did suggest that I shouldn't tell my older son that his father had died, as he was so young and would soon forget him. But I needed him to understand that his beloved daddy did not leave of his own volition. It was hard, but utterly necessary.

'Do you have any other children?' A bereaved friend was asked this question. When she replied that yes, she had four others, her inquisitor said, oh, that was all right then – as if in those circumstances she really wouldn't miss one.

'Do you have any children?' This is a killer question for those of us who have lost a child, and the reply can explode like a bomb, especially in social situations. I advise people to rehearse the answer they want to give to protect themselves. I am very private about my life and will never disclose anything unless I feel that I know and trust the person I am speaking with. It has been very difficult for me to write this account and share feelings that have been private to me for so long. Some who feel they know me well do not know that my son died and would be amazed to read what I have written. One of the hardest things I had to cope with following the deaths of my father, my husband and my son was the loss of myself. I became the girl whose father had died, the widow with the two small children, the woman whose son had been killed. But in the middle of all this was me, and I was being lost.

'How can I help?' An offer of genuine help is invaluable, but if you say it, you must back it up with action. The bereaved do not need people who are long on promises but short on keeping to them. Specify what you are prepared to do and keep to it.

'You should go and see your GP.' The sub-text here is: 'I can't deal with your grief and you must need medication.' Perhaps that is so, but I have learned that some members of the clinical professions have few skills to offer the grieving – and GPs are among them. When my husband and then my son died, I did not think that I was depressed. I personally subscribe to the psychologist Dorothy Rowe's thoughts on grief and bereavement. What we are experiencing is deep, deep sorrow and sadness. While antidepressants are necessary for some, they can blunt our real feelings and delay the process of recovery.

'I don't know what to say.' This is all that needs to be said, and is the most acceptable set of words. There is nothing else that can be said, and it gives the bereaved person room to speak about what has happened and be listened to. Listening is the most valuable gift to give those bereaved.

Following the death of his son, Rabbi Harold Kushner (1992) wrote about people telling him how sensitive and effective he had become as a pastor since his son, Aaron, had died – and how he would give all this up to be the ordinary rabbi he had been before and have his son back.

But we cannot choose. It is now 22 years since my son was killed and here I am, still carrying the elephant. Kevin is always in my heart.

For Michael, my mother and my brother and my closest friend April. You made my journey possible.

Further reading

Cruse Bereavement Care promotes the well-being of bereaved people and enables anyone of whatever age who has been bereaved by death to understand their grief and cope with their loss. Cruse is the UK's largest bereavement charity. See <www.crusebereavementcare. org.uk>; helpline 0844 477 9400.

Should you need to read more on the subject, the most useful reference I have found is: Harriet Sarnoff Schiff (2008), *The Bereaved Parent*, London: Souvenir Press. I can also strongly recommend Julie Nicholson (2010), *A Song for Jenny*, London: HarperCollins.

References

Kushner, H. S. (1992), *When Bad Things Happen to Good People*, London: Pan.

O'Casey, Sean (1991). *Niall: A lament*, London: Calder.

Rosen, M. (2002), *Carrying the Elephant: A Memoir of Love and Loss*, London: Penguin.

Tonkin, L. (1996), 'Growing around Grief – Another Way of Looking at Grief and Recovery', *Bereavement Care*, 15(1):10.

4

Changing cultures of grief, 1850–1970: from Archbishop Tait to C. S. Lewis

PAT JALLAND

Fifty years ago C. S. Lewis's book, *A Grief Observed* (Lewis, 1964), became a bestseller among bereaved people, and it still has a profound impact today. This book was unique in the half century of silence about death and bereavement in England following the First World War. In contrast, the widely read book of consolation published by Archbishop Tait in 1879, over 80 years earlier, is forgotten today. Tait's memorial volume on the deaths of his wife and six children (Benham, 1879) also proved remarkably popular, selling 12,000 copies in its first year. Tait's book was the nineteenth-century equivalent of Lewis's *A Grief Observed*. These two consolation volumes describe experiences of grief in the 1850s and 1960s, over a century apart.

Lewis's and Tait's accounts of grieving experiences were written in two contrasting cultural and social worlds. Cultural norms relating to grief have shifted dramatically in England over the past 150 years, shaped powerfully by the decline of religion, the two world wars, demographic change and the medical revolution. This essay explores these themes and draws on my recent book, *Death in War and Peace: A History of Loss and Grief in England, 1914–1970* (Jalland, 2010) and my earlier book, *Death in the Victorian Family* (Jalland, 1998). These books were informed by unpublished letters and diaries and other primary sources in English archives, so vital in a new field of historical study. They documented in detail a gradual change from a dominant Christian culture of open acceptance of death and grief in England in the 1850s to avoidance and reticence a century later.

Religion played a powerful role in the lives of most middle- and upper-class Victorians, for whom church attendance was usually more than just a matter of convention, and half the working classes still attended church in 1851. From the late eighteenth century the Evangelical movement strengthened Christianity in England. Large elements of the population were affected by the Evangelical impulses of seriousness, piety, discipline and duty, which brought families into close contact with God through Bible study and family prayers. Evangelicalism reached the peak of its social and spiritual influence in the 1850s and 1860s, starting to decline from the 1870s. It had been called 'the religion of the heart', encouraging men as well as women to show the intensity of their grief on the deaths of loved ones by weeping together. Death evoked intense emotions, often expressed through the art, literature and poetry of the Romantic movement that largely coincided with the Evangelical revival (Best, 1970, pp. 50–5).

The Evangelical movement had enormous influence on death-bed behaviour through its revival of the medieval Christian ideal of the 'good death' among the middle and upper classes. It required piety and lifelong preparation, as well as fortitude in the face of physical suffering. The good death should ideally take place in a good Christian home, surrounded by a loving family, with the dying person achieving worthiness for salvation, comforted by the assurance of a family reunion in heaven. Family members were expected to be emotionally and physically involved with their dying loved one – weeping, holding and stroking, and writing detailed accounts of the dying days and hours. However, it was more difficult in life than in idealized art or literature to achieve the Evangelical good death, and it was almost impossible for the poor and unbelievers. Realization of the ideal varied enormously according to class, age, gender, religion, family circumstances, and the nature of the disease.

Mourning rituals help to meet the psychological needs of the bereaved by structuring death within an accepted system of values, while rallying the support of family, friends and community to comfort the bereaved. Victorian rituals provided vital opportunities for bereaved people to express their sorrow in a manner that made the grieving experience more meaningful and easier to endure. Protestant Christianity still provided the dominant belief system to console the bereaved. The funeral began the process of working through grief, affirming the reality of the loss through public recognition of the death and gathering together family, friends and community to share the sorrow.

If the supreme Christian consolation on the death of a loved one was the belief in the resurrection of the body, then the continuing memory of the deceased was almost equally important, to believers and unbelievers alike. The bereaved might find comfort in repeatedly talking through memories, especially with relatives and friends who knew the deceased. The Victorians understood the significant role of visible symbols of remembrance in their grieving process. They perpetuated the memory of dead loved ones in paintings, photographs, death-masks and busts, as well as through monuments, mourning jewellery and grave-visiting. The grave in the cemetery became a site for remembrance, meditation and consolation for many Victorian families, helping to evoke a sense of closeness to the dead loved one.

Such rituals doubtless helped many bereaved people, but they could not cure the 'anguish of the soul' for parents of children who died. The death of a child was usually the most distressing loss of all, but such deaths were a common fact of life for all classes in Victorian England. The grim statistics for

54

infant mortality record a high death rate throughout the nine-teenth century, with little change until after 1900. Over 100,000 infants a year died before their first birthday – one-quarter of all babies. Every mother had to face the possibility that at least one child would die at birth or soon after. All classes were affected, but poor working-class children in large industrial cities such as Liverpool and Manchester suffered most. The turning point in this appalling child mortality rate was not reached until 1906, when a slow decline in the death rate commenced, largely caused by a dramatic reduction in deaths from infectious diseases, which mainly affected the young.

For many nineteenth-century English families the death of a child was the supreme test of Christian faith. For Archibald Tait, Dean of Carlisle and later Archbishop of Canterbury, the deaths in 1856 of five of his six children led to a highly emotional struggle to accept God's will. Tait's five little girls died one by one, within two months, during an epidemic of virulent scarlet fever, for which there was then no cure. The heartbroken parents each wrote lengthy journal accounts of their catastrophe: 'it was a sight full of agony. The conflict with death was long' for each little girl. The parents suffered anguish as they watched by each deathbed in turn: 'they are hours which burn into one's soul . . . our hearts are well nigh broken' (Tait, 1856).

The parents' detailed diaries of over 130 pages each revealed the 'unspeakable agony' and 'deepest darkness' of their supreme test of Christian faith. Both parents had a simple belief that death signified a transition to a happier world with God, where they would eventually be reunited. Yet each experienced a profound struggle to reach complete submission to God's will. On many days they 'wept together for our darlings', as they contemplated a future without them. They ultimately found solace in their belief that their daughters had joined Christ and were rescued from a sinful and suffering world. The overarch-ing consolation for both parents was the prospect of a future reunion with their beloved daughters, 'when we shall meet to part no more'.

However, Archibald Tait's grief was longer lasting and more complicated than that of his wife, Catharine. Despite her long struggle, Catharine had been trained from childhood to be submissive, both as a Christian and as an obedient woman. There was a clear gendered difference. By contrast, her husband's battle was prolonged by his deeper sense of divine retribution: he regarded his suffering on his children's deaths as punishment for his own sin. In this Dean Tait's ordeal was in some respects more like that of C. S. Lewis than Catharine Tait.

For both Tait parents the Carlisle tragedy was a lifelong sorrow, exacerbated in 1878 by the death of their only son, a loss that Catharine found literally unbearable. She died suddenly six months later. Archibald, Archbishop of Canterbury from 1869, was devastated: 'As time wears on I feel more and more desolate.' His submissive response to the 'two awful trials' was seen as an example to others: he was venerated as a man set apart by his profound experience of suffering. Other bereaved parents assured the Archbishop that his strength was 'a help and blessing' to thousands of parents all over the world.

Catharine Tait's powerful emotional narrative of her daughters' deaths in 1856 and her successful struggle to submit to God's will was discovered in her papers after her own death. Published by the Archbishop as a memorial volume in 1879, with over 12,000 copies printed in the first year alone, it was one of the most widely read Victorian books of consolation literature, and letters of thanks poured in from bereaved parents who found it helped them cope with devastating grief. Sarah Jones of Liverpool was one of many who wrote to the Archbishop about the death of her own four children from scarlet fever: Catharine Tait's story 'affords my stricken heart some consolation'. Such outpourings of grief served as therapy for the writer, easing the pain of grief and supplying a measure of peace. For the families who treasured these accounts they sustained their sense of closeness to the deceased, as well as helping them through the grieving process.

Such public memorials of children's deaths in the nineteenth century depended for their value on two cultural foundations. They spoke to an age when many people experienced the loss of children, and their primary message of consolation was that of Christian faith, reinforced by supportive rituals and warm family sympathy. Their strong religious faith and everyday practice of Christianity, supported by this rich language of consolation, gave the bereaved a powerful structure for coping with death.

Although Archbishop Tait's memorial to his dead family was in some respects the Victorian equivalent of C. S. Lewis's *A Grief Observed*, there was a huge social and cultural gulf between them, for several reasons. First, a dramatic new demographic pattern was established from about 1870, whereby the death rate in England and Wales fell from 22 per thousand per year in 1868 to 14.8 in 1908 and 11.7 in 1928. The high-water mark of Victorian mortality had already been reached when Tait's book of consolation was published. This decline in mortality can be explained by public health reforms, better diet and living standards and the natural reduction in mortality from infectious diseases. Life expectancy at birth in England and Wales increased from about 40 years in 1850 to 52 for males and 55 for females by 1911–12. Thus between 1850 and 1918 the most common time of death began to shift from infancy to old age. Within half a century death began to be perceived as the monopoly of the elderly, and society's preoccupation with death receded.

The gradual decline in Christian faith between 1850 and 1918 was the second fundamental motor of change in the English history of death, grief and mourning. The doubts experienced by Archbishop Tait while his daughters were dying reflected the spirit of the age. Victorians faced the combined theoretical challenges of biblical criticism, geological discoveries and

Darwinian evolutionary theory, as well as profound economic and social changes. Religious doubt was insidious but the process was slow and gradual. From the 1870s church attendance ceased to keep pace with population growth, and the immense power of the Evangelical revival had passed its peak by the 1880s.

Late-Victorian unbelievers could be isolated in their grief in an age when Christianity was still dominant, lacking both the faith and the church support that sustained Christians. Unbelievers also rejected Christian faith and rituals, and the biblical language of consolation, but had not yet developed alternative strategies for coping with grief. Charles Darwin's letters of condolence to bereaved friends indicate his inability to express his own sorrow or offer much sympathy to others. His letters were terse, stilted and embarrassed, in contrast to the warmly emotional letters of many Victorian Christians, including his own wife. Darwin had lost the Victorian language for expressing such sympathy when he slowly surrendered his faith. His wife, Emma Darwin, remained a committed Evangelical Christian and must have found their difference in faith distressing, especially as they were rarely, if ever, able to discuss it. It was difficult to sustain two different languages of grief and condolence, especially on the terrible death of their beloved child, Annie, at the age of ten in 1851, possibly from typhoid (Barlow, 1958, pp. 85–95).

Thomas Huxley privately acknowledged in 1893 that his unusual views on religion and death separated him from Victorian society, leaving him isolated: he was 'hopelessly at variance' with most of his fellow-men in his agnosticism. On the death of his three-year-old son, Noel, Huxley's unbelief was severely tested. But he stood firm in his view that immortality was a 'mischievous delusion', and death was final. Believers held awful fears for agnostics and atheists obliged to face 'the utter grimness of a death unbrightened by faith' (Huxley, 1900). Agnostics lacked a substitute for Christian rituals of consolation and its support network. The consequence could be a terrible isolation in bereavement, 'a solitude beyond the reach of God or man', in the resonant phrase of the poet William Blunt.

However, we should not overstate the decline in religious faith in the late nineteenth century. Certainly there was a reduction in Evangelical fervour and church attendance ceased to keep pace with population growth, but religion remained powerful among the respectable classes. Jose Harris suggests that the predominant religion of these years was 'an undogmatic "social" Christianity' (Harris, 1993, pp. 253, 171–2, 179). The doctrines of hell and judgement were slowly eroded from the 1850s, and the popular view of heaven was increasingly as a happy home of family reunions. But the process of secularization was slow, and is far from complete today.

Moreover, expression of grief in the late nineteenth century varied according to class, gender and region, as well as religion. Historian Julie-Marie Strange has reconstructed a working-class culture of grief, often expressed through silences and symbolic rituals rather than overt emotion and formal language. Poverty and high mortality rates did not foster indifference so much as resignation and careful restraint in emotions. Distressed mothers might hide intense grief on the deaths of children, displaying little overt affection. Even so, a vital working-class culture of grief survived into the 1940s and beyond, especially in the north of England and the Celtic fringe, and in rural areas. Emphasis was placed on the rituals of care of the corpse, viewing the dead and communal wakes (Strange, 2005, pp. 195, 254–5).

Whereas religious faith was a dominant force in the history of death and grief in nineteenth-century England, after 1914 it became one of several important variables, playing a less influential role. Instead, the two world wars, demographic change and the medical revolution became more fundamental forces for change in the twentieth-century history of bereavement. The striking new demographic pattern that started about 1870, with a continuous decline in mortality from infectious diseases and increased life expectancy, was intensified from 1935 onwards, when the sulphonamide drugs and penicillin revolutionized modern medicine and vastly increased doctors' power to cure. The loss of a patient came to represent failure, and death and grief became topics to be evaded. Moreover, death increasingly moved from family control at home to hospitals that were concerned with medical and technical efficiency to prolong life.

Above all, the two world wars had a profound and cumulative impact on the prolonged transformation of responses to grief in the 50 years after 1914. During the First World War the military culture required that soldiers repress their emotions and respond in silence to appalling experiences. The numbers and nature of soldiers' deaths were horrific and communal grief overwhelming. But there were powerful pressures for both soldiers and their families at home to remain stoical and silent about their personal losses. Indeed, in letters home, serving sons and husbands urged their families to be brave if they died and to grieve for them in silence. The *Barnsley Chronicle* was confident in 1916 that the massive sacrifices at the Battle of the Somme would be borne with 'Spartan courage' by the brave women of Barnsley, in the national interest. They must show the same bravery as their men at the front. The emotional constraints for women could be more challenging than for men, as their responses to death and loss in the preceding century had often been more expressive.

Some soldiers sought comfort in faith on the loss of comrades, but religion only aided a minority. The urban working classes, other than the Catholics, had deserted many churches, especially in the north, and many poor had never really belonged. By 1920, 60 per cent of English people were nominally Anglicans, 15 per cent Free Church, and 5 per cent Roman Catholic – the Anglicans stronger in the south and the others in the north. Up to 50 per cent of the population had no meaningful religious affiliation, especially the unskilled urban working classes in the north. Of perhaps greater concern to the churches from 1920 was the prolonged slow decline in Christian faith among their core congregation, the middle classes, as more moved towards agnosticism (Hastings, 2001, pp. 104–7, 266–72).

In 1919 Bishop E. S. Talbot chaired a committee of inquiry into 'The Army and Religion', which concluded that the working classes had been falling away from the churches since the Industrial Revolution, but that 'many soldiers were in some measure Christian without knowing it'. A major stumbling block for the soldiers was their difficulty in reconciling a loving God with the indiscriminate suffering and mass deaths of the Great War. Fatalism, folk religion and supernatural belief made more sense to many soldiers than Christianity, as they helped soldiers come to terms with the terrifying experiences of trench warfare. Many soldiers combined a nebulous faith in God with a belief in the paranormal, including spiritualism, which offered the hope of contacting the fallen and the assurance that the dead of the Great War lived on (Wilkinson, 1978, pp. 160–1, 233–4, 260).

The Talbot inquiry also found that the Church of England lacked the necessary sacramental rituals to enable soldiers to cope adequately with the prospect of death and grief for fallen comrades. By contrast, Roman Catholic chaplains could offer comforting rituals of confession and absolution before a battle and extreme unction to the dying. There were only about two million Catholics in England and Wales in 1920 but their numbers increased rapidly from the 1940s, with further Irish immigration and large numbers of East European Catholic migrants. The appeal of the Catholic Church, in peace as in war, lay in its claims to authority, as well as its realism and its comforting sacramental system.

Indeed, in the 50 years after the Great War there was a complex shift from a Victorian culture where death was often accepted and grief openly expressed, to a culture of avoidance, minimal ritual and private sorrow. The mass slaughter of the war brought intense communal grief and a powerful reaction against Victorian ways of death. David Cannadine has argued that inter-war England was obsessed by the cult of the dead in the face of widespread and harrowing bereavement. Victorian death practices seemed inadequate and inappropriate, particularly in the absence of the bodies buried on the battlefields. Traditional mourning rituals were unable to cope and declined dramatically during the war. Soldiers' burial in England had been prohibited, so grieving families had no funerals or graves at home as a focus for sorrow. Victorian-style deathbeds and ritualized mourning were impossible. So new innovative ways were devised to remember the dead – the remarkable rituals at the Cenotaph, the Armistice Day commemoration and local civic war memorials erected across the country (Cannadine, 1981, pp. 187–242).

This national project of commemoration for the war dead may have come at some private cost, in that traditional mourning rituals for civilians in peacetime declined even further after the war. Perhaps also the grand scale of national commemoration overshadowed and limited public compassion for the ordinary deaths of individual civilians in peacetime. The inter-war generation grew up in a bleak atmosphere of mass mourning for the dead soldiers of the Great War. Even the 200,000 victims of the influenza pandemic of 1918–19 received little of the attention reserved for the war heroes. This foreshadowed the silences surrounding death and grief in peacetime, in the inter-war years and beyond. Prolonged deathbed scenes disappeared and bereavement rituals declined in length, fervour and consolation.

Yet we must not overstate the extent of this decline in ritual and commemoration for civilians in peacetime in the inter-war years. In the north of England, the Midlands and the Celtic fringe there were powerful continuities with the working-class culture of death and grieving in the late nineteenth century described by Julie-Marie Strange. Older traditions were often remarkably resilient in these areas, particularly among the lower working classes, women and older people. Elizabeth Roberts has shown that spiritual beliefs and long-established rituals were still strong among women in Preston, Lancaster and Barrow, where continuity with the past was powerful. A respected neighbourhood layer-out washed the body, which was kept in an open coffin in the front parlour, as kin and neighbours paid their last respects. A 'good send-off' at a crowded funeral allowed the living to confront the reality of death and start the grieving process. The funeral tea was a time for family solidarity and comforting reminiscences before months of mourning when the community grieved and the dead were 'constantly remembered' (Roberts, 1989, pp. 188–207). From the 1940s, death was increasingly removed from the community of women by doctors and funeral directors and many old rituals were attenuated. However, the rate of change varied greatly by class and region: some rituals survived among the northern working classes into the 1960s and beyond, especially in more isolated regions.

The Second World War marked a deeper break with the past than the Great War and the process was cumulative. A pervasive model of silence about death and of suppressed grieving became entrenched in the English psyche. Churchill called for courage and stoicism during the German air blitz on British cities. The dark side of the blitz story was sanitized to sustain morale in the interests of survival. But mass bereavement tended to devalue the grief of individuals. During the war the defence forces again provided the stoical model for the country to follow, with the celebrated stiff upper lip, the resolve to conceal emotion, and the silent suffering of bereaved relatives. The government encouraged civilians not to dwell on the intense distress of individual bereaved people.

One story of the grief of a soldier's traumatized father is valuable because it is so rare in a culture of wartime silence about bereavement. During the Second World War Professor Geoffrey Bickersteth lost his beloved son Julian in Greece, reviving memories of the death of Geoffrey's brother Morris at the

Somme in 1916. Geoffrey had two daughters and three sons: he lost Julian in January 1945, killed by a stray shell while he was off duty on the final day of the Greek civil war. The chance nature of Julian's death was subsequently compounded by the death of Geoffrey's eldest son Tony, when he was struck by lightning on holiday in Italy in 1947. Geoffrey's Christian faith was severely tested by the 'utter purposelessness' of both sons' deaths. His grief was movingly recorded in a series of intense letters to his blind aged mother, Ella, who had earlier been a pilgrim to her son's grave in a Great War cemetery (Bickersteth, n.d.; Jalland, 2010, pp. 166–71).

Geoffrey Bickersteth largely internalized his emotional devastation on Julian's death, discussing it little, even with his wife Jean: 'One has no business to spread one's own sorrows, especially when . . . tens of thousands of others are suffering in silence far worse pain than we are.' His wife generously fulfilled the prevailing cultural prescription of a brave grieving mother, suppressing her emotions as far as possible, even in private. The dichotomy here is pronounced: Geoffrey obeyed the cultural expectation of emotional constraint within the community and even in his own family, but felt compelled to pour out his grief privately to his aged mother, who understood only too well the pain of losing a son to war.

Geoffrey Bickersteth's strong Christian faith was severely challenged by his loss. He knew he should be unselfish enough not to resent his son's removal to a heavenly future of joy and vitality, but he resented God for blighting his own future, especially as a father should die before a son. Geoffrey's anger against God was perhaps predictable, as anger is a common component of grief and God was a natural target for a deeply religious man. The celebration of Easter Day in 1945, in the fourth month of bereavement, forced Geoffrey to confront the challenge to his faith. He sat with his family at the Easter service at Aberdeen Cathedral, hoping for a message of comfort. Instead it was 'a complete wash-out . . . comfort comes in the next world not this'. Expectation of reunion with Julian in heaven did little to compensate for the loss of the real Julian in the flesh: 'Julian in paradise might just as well be non-existent ... It's exhausting, is grief.' But in the next few months Geoffrey could reflect more positively that his faith had never been extinguished, even when he was 'desperately depressed'. Ultimately he knew his faith would reconcile him to his son's death, though he would always miss him: 'one carries on ... but the thrill has gone, irrevocably'. Throughout such intense grief his immediate family 'says little about it'. The second ordeal of the death of Geoffrey's eldest son, Tony, was another sore trial of faith – to reconcile death by lightning with a loving God. But once again grief was borne with silent courage as the dead sons might have wished.

The change in cultural norms affecting death and grief in England was more intense and long-lasting from the 1940s. The community coped with the huge losses of both wars by a complex mixture of remembering and forgetting, which are also contradictory aspects of the grief process itself. Across much of the English community in the 20 years after 1945, open and expressive sorrow was more strongly discouraged in favour of suppressed privatized grieving. The gender gap was reduced as women internalized their sorrow and moved closer to a traditionally male pattern of grieving. The wars had made emotional restraint the customary code for all, regardless of gender. Women had understood during the war that it was self-indulgent 'to spread one's own sorrows' when thousands of others were suffering in silence. They must hide their feelings: 'you do your mourning quietly, alone. The same as you might do praying.' This shift in female patterns of grieving was a major contributor to the pervasive culture of silence about death and grief from the 1940s. The traditional English reserve about expression of emotions was enhanced by the two wars, especially the second (Jalland, 2010, chs 7–8).

In the 15 or more years after 1945 the culture of grief was characterized by silence, as bereaved people lacked guidelines to help them cope with the loss of family and friends. It is impossible to appreciate today how widespread and deep-rooted was the ignorance, silence and embarrassment about grief in the 1950s and 1960s, and how pervasive the advice to keep busy and move on. Psychiatrists had not yet constructed theories of grief helpful to the wider society, and there were no bereavement counsellors or advice books explaining what to expect and how to cope. Bereaved people were advised to keep busy, pretend to be cheerful and grieve privately in silence.

Widows suffered in silence and received little community support. One war widow was stunned by widowhood at the age of 27 – 'I felt completely at sea' – but she felt obliged 'to put on a good show' because the community was not interested in her grief. In 1959 Margaret Torrie, a Quaker, and her psychiatrist husband Alfred, established the Cruse Bereavement Care organization to offer advice and comfort to widows who felt utterly isolated, as people avoided the subjects of death and grief. One widow found Cruse a great comfort as she had never known a bereaved person and had no idea that grief was so painful (Bowlby, n.d.). There was considerable emphasis in Cruse's earlier years on Christian consolation, but by the 1990s it had become mainly secular: psychological counselling and well-tested grief theories largely replaced religious faith.

A transformation in English cultural norms began in the 1960s, sometimes called 'the expressive revolution', which helped to alter the pervasive silence and ignorance about grief. Significant changes in the cultural, intellectual and social climate encouraged more liberal attitudes and greater freedom of emotional expression, especially for women. The middle-class caring professions were strongly affected, and the process also influenced broader cultural assumptions and values. Some of the churches' former functions in pastoral care and bereavement support were gradually taken over by psychiatrists, social workers and secular caring professionals. But these changes should not be over-stated. Those affected were likely to be educated middle-class people from the cities, large towns and the south. By contrast, white working-class families in the north, the Celtic fringe and rural areas were more likely to retain vestiges of their traditional rituals of mourning. The changes were slow, but the 1960s and 1970s can be seen as turning points.

Such cultural change was powerfully encouraged by the personal contribution of C. S. Lewis, whose book, *A Grief Observed*, was first published anonymously in 1961. Lewis's book was a complex analysis of his own experience of grief on the death of his beloved American wife, Joy. Lewis had been one of the leaders in a period of spiritual revival and literary creativity after the war. His own works included *The Screwtape Letters*, which sold more than a million copies, making him a household name in the 1950s. He combined uncompromising faith with accessible scholarship and literary creativity. It is a reflection on the profound silence of the culture of death and grief in the 1950s and 1960s that even Lewis had seen no need before his own bereavement to explain the meaning of grief in his correspondence and his books, as he had that of pain.

Lewis had bottled up his emotions for years following his mother's early death and a tough boarding school upbringing. From 1925 he spent 30 years as a Fellow in English literature at Oxford, and finally at Cambridge. He was charmed by the lively American writer Joy Gresham in 1952 and finally married her in 1957, when she was suffering from terminal bone cancer. On her death in July 1960 Lewis was in a state of 'psychological paralysis'. *A Grief Observed* was written in the months after Joy's death, taking us intimately inside his own grief as he experienced it day by day. It demonstrates the trauma and complexities that a profound religious faith could add to the experience of grief. Lewis's little book was an attempt to 'make a map of sorrow' – to describe his own experience of grieving in as detached a manner as possible. Lewis depicted his grief as an ever-changing journey along an endless winding road, with a new landscape at every turn. Grief was utterly unpredictable, full of alternating despair and pain. Lewis's account was in many respects similar to the diary kept by Archibald Tait in 1856 as his daughters were dying, and also to Geoffrey Bickersteth's letters of grief on his son's death in 1945. Lewis's book, like Tait's, became a popular guide to grief for many years.

For Lewis, compiling his account acted as a safety valve against total collapse: he commenced it because his need was desperate and little other emotional support was available in the cultural climate of 1960. Lewis wrote:

> I'm aware of being an embarrassment to everyone I meet. At work, at the club, in the street, I see people, as they approach me, trying to make up their minds whether they'll 'say something about it' or not. Some funk it altogether . . . Perhaps the bereaved ought to be isolated in special settlements like lepers.

Some well-wishers tried to reassure Lewis that his wife was with God, but this suggestion opened up an appalling struggle as his grief adversely affected his view of God and seemed to question the foundation of his faith. During the first two months of grief he tortured himself with the fear that God must be cruel to allow Joy such appalling suffering. Later still, he wondered why no one had ever explained that grief was wayward and awful. But Lewis was experiencing grief at a time of deep cultural reticence, when social scientists had barely started drawing the 'map of sorrow' he sought. He also experienced a prolonged conflict between an impossible desire to return to his past life with his dead wife and the need to build a new life without her (Lewis, 1964).

Following months of terrible anguish he was finally able to see his wife as part of his spiritual communion with God. He survived a fundamental crisis of faith by understanding that 'Joy and all the dead are like God. In that respect loving her has become . . . like loving Him' (Lewis, 1964). Lewis survived his wife by just three years, dying in 1963, his faith intact, aged only 65. After Lewis's death, *A Grief Observed* was republished in his own name, and itself contributed to the changing cultural climate influencing bereavement. His book became a bestseller, and helped thousands of bereaved people in the following decades, especially in Britain and the United States. The poet W. H. Auden, like countless others, considered it the best first-hand account of grief he had ever read. T. S. Eliot described it as 'intensely moving'.

Perhaps C. S. Lewis's famous book encouraged the Christian churches to strengthen their spiritual leadership in relation to bereaved people from the 1960s. Institutional religion held its own more effectively than its critics predicted. There had been a renewal of Protestant religious culture between the 1940s and 1960s, and a Catholic revival from the 1960s. The Methodist churches and the Church of England experienced slow decline thereafter, but there were several growth areas. The Catholic Church substantially increased its numbers through European immigration, and still retained the advantage of its sacramental ritual, so comforting to the dying and bereaved. As the national church, the Church of England retained links with many irregular churchgoers, while its evangelical wing appealed to younger people and to immigrants from Africa and the Caribbean. The medical sociologist David Clark has emphasized the continuing influence of 'folk religion' in response to bereavement in the later twentieth century. He describes it as a rich combination of church faith, unorthodox beliefs and superstition, including faith in God and some kind of afterlife (Clark, 1982, passim).

Modern psychology had contributed relatively little advice about the normal processes of grieving before the 1960s. The eminent psychiatrist Dr Colin Murray Parkes' classic 1972 book, *Bereavement*, was not a personal narrative like those of Archbishop Tait or C. S. Lewis. It drew on his empirical pioneering research and sustained clinical work over decades. Dr Parkes' book was a unique and influential professional account that described in detail the manifestations of grieving and emphasized that they varied significantly between individuals: 'grief is a painful process of change, by which someone gradually gives up one world and enters another'. Forty years later *Bereavement* has been frequently reprinted and has stood the test of time, offering vital information, advice and reassurance to numerous bereaved people (Parkes, 1972, 2000).

Since 1972 a substantial and sometimes complex theoretical literature on grief has been published by social scientists, with an emphasis on diversity rather than prescriptive stages. Experts over the last four decades have suggested that bereaved people may express their sorrow in many ways. Moreover, patterns of grieving behaviour may change over time and across gender: indeed, the present essay has amply demonstrated the historical accuracy of these observations. Psychologist Paul Rosenblatt (1993) observed that grief is shaped by its social context: 'cultures differ widely in defining death and in defining what is an appropriate expression of grief'. Margaret Stroebe and Henk Schut (1999) suggested that there was not a universal process of grief with fixed stages. Rather, we should see healthy grieving as an oscillation between dwelling on the death and loss on the one hand, and dealing with the practical consequences and future possibilities on the other. Such theories are today passed on to bereaved people by grief counsellors and practical popular advice manuals. We have come a long way from the anguish of the war widows and other bereaved people in the 1940s and 1950s who were frightened and isolated in a society that offered little support and no advice.

Another change since the 1970s has been the revival of expressive grieving, led principally by middle-class women. This has involved a significant reversal of the pattern over the previous half-century, when women were encouraged to imitate men's more constrained grieving behaviour. This change in cultural norms was a response to the women's movement and the 'expressive revolution' of the 1960s, noted earlier. Expressive grieving was encouraged by the popular bereavement counselling movement, especially Cruse counsellors for widows, who worked through the phases of grief in groups or one-to-one sessions, emphasizing the value of weeping and talking freely about the dead person.

Mutual help groups such as Compassionate Friends, a support organization for bereaved parents, share the belief that expressive forms of grieving are helpful, but they approach it differently. They see themselves as communities in which common experiences of loss can best be shared with others suffering in the same way. The oral testimony of Val Hazel (1991) describes the support she found in a mutual help group after her nine-year-old son Jeff died from a rare brain tumour in 1976. After the funeral, Val was aware that people outside the family tried to avoid her because they didn't know what to say, and thought that she should grieve quietly at home. But Val needed to talk about Jeff and she found the ideal outlet for her feelings in sharing her sorrow with other bereaved parents she had met at St Bartholomew's Hospital. She was in touch with many such parents 'all in the same boat . . . And it wasn't all doom and gloom.' Other people who had suffered in the same way could sometimes help more than family or friends.

Another valuable expressive response to bereavement has been the revival since the 1970s of the nineteenth-century custom of publishing narratives of personal experiences of grief. For example, Compassionate Friends published stories and poems about children who had died, as 'a living memorial' to acknowledge the continuing presence of those beloved children in their lives. Some bereaved people hope to make a shattering and confused experience coherent and meaningful, or simply to share their varied experiences. Above all they seek to ensure the subject of grief will no longer be hidden, as it was when C. S. Lewis composed his own searing account. Some narratives stress the normality of grief and others explore its complexity and diversity in order to find its meaning. A long, painful journey of grief can be transformed into a pilgrimage of personal growth. In this way the Victorian tradition of the grief narrative has survived many decades of cultural silence (see e.g. Dickenson, 2000, pp. 347–70).

References

Barlow, N., ed. (1958), *The Autobiography of Charles Darwin, 1809–1882*, London: Collins.

Benham, W., ed. (1879), *Catharine and Crawford Tait, Wife and Son of Archbishop A. C. Tait: A Memoir*.

Best, G. (1970), 'Evangelicalism and the Victorians', in Anthony Symondson, ed., *The Victorian Crisis of Faith*, London: SPCK.

Bickersteth Papers, MS Eng. E.3150, Bodleian Library, Oxford.

Bowlby, J., 'The World of the Widow', Bowlby Papers, PP/BOW/F5/1/box 41, Wellcome Institute.

Cannadine, D. (1981), 'War, Death and Mourning in Modern Britain', in Joachim Whaley, ed., *Mirrors of Mortality*, London: Europa.

Clark, D. (1982), *Between Pulpit and Pew: Folk Religion in a North Yorkshire Fishing Village*, Cambridge: CUP.

Dickenson, D. et al., eds (2000), *Death, Dying and Bereavement*, 2nd edn, London: Sage.

Harris, J. (1993), *Private Lives, Public Spirit: A Social History of Britain 1870–1914*, Oxford: OUP.

Hastings, A. (2001), *A History of English Christianity, 1900–2000*, rev. edn, London: SCM Press.

Hazel, V. (1991), interview in *Perspective for Living*, H 913/04, British Library.

Huxley, L. (1900), *The Life and Letters of Thomas Henry Huxley*, 2 vols.

Jalland, P. (1998), *Death in the Victorian Family*, Oxford: OUP.

Jalland, P. (2010), *Death in War and Peace: A History of Loss and Grief in England, 1914–1970*, Oxford: OUP.

Lewis, C. S. (1964), *A Grief Observed*, London: Faber & Faber.

Parkes, C. M. (1972), *Bereavement: Studies of Grief in Adult Life*, 1st edn, London: Tavistock Press.

Parkes, C. M. (2000), 'Bereavement as a psychological transition', in Donna Dickenson et al., eds (2000), *Death, Dying and Bereavement*, London: Sage.

Roberts, E. (1989), 'The Lancashire Way of Death', in Ralph Houlbrooke, ed., *Death, Ritual and Bereavement*, London: Routledge.

Rosenblatt, P. C. (1993), 'Grief: The Social Context of Private Feelings', in Margaret Stroebe et al., eds, *Handbook of Bereavement*, Cambridge: CUP.

Strange, J.-M. (2005), *Death, Grief and Poverty in Britain, 1870–1914*, Cambridge: CUP.

Stroebe, M. and Schut, H. (1999), 'The Dual Process Model of Coping with Bereavement', *Death Studies*, 23.

Tait, Dean A. C. (1856), Journal on the deaths of his children, Tait Papers, vol. 39, fos. 1–128, Lambeth Palace Library.

Wilkinson, A. (1978), *The Church of England and the First World War*, London: SPCK.

5

How do you do what you do? Loss and mourning in a professional context

SUE SMITH AND JONATHAN MARTIN

Introduction

Frank (1995) suggests that there is more to experience about illness and dying than a medical or psychological story can tell. We would agree. And so we intend in this chapter to provide 'rich' rather than 'thin' accounts (White, 2007) of our experience of working with people who are dying, acknowledging that it is not only the professional context of exploration that informs us and can be used as a resource, but multiple contexts: our lived experiences, our backgrounds and the circumstances that inform and influence us – age, experiences of loss, stories and beliefs about death, dying and mourning, gender, religion and so on. In this we are influenced by a systemic perspective where we are invited to focus on relationships, rather than individuals, to view expertise as located in those seeking help and to join people in their contexts and respectfully engage with other practitioners or people using our services 'in relation to their pains, joy, sufferings and creative potential' (Lang, Little and Cronen, 1990, p. 38). We are not, therefore, presenting a manual of 'how to do it' – which can sometimes be helpful but often is not – as to do such a thing suggests that we can position ourselves in our work as 'already knowing', which can potentially create distance between ourselves and those we intend to help and prevent us from listening to them (Riikonen, 1999). Nor does it capture the richness, variety and complexity of our work. And so we move away from a 'rational knowing that' and 'knowing what', that is, that predetermined theories and knowledge can tell us what to do with an individual/family/team and how to behave, to a relational knowing, and the idea that we can know from our own contexts and the contexts of those we intend to help and that there is a reciprocity between the two (Shotter, 1993).

We were struck through the course of our conversations in preparation for writing this chapter by our shared experience of friends, family members, colleagues and those we help at work frequently saying, 'How do you do what you do?' frequently followed by, 'Isn't it a bit gloomy and depressing?' followed in turn by a sigh. Implied in these comments is the idea that our work is tough, something only certain people can engage with; it is outside the mainstream. Perhaps it is also a thank you, an acknowledgement of the 'difficult work we do' (Smith and Hennessey, 2009). And yet, are people really seeking an answer to this question? Perhaps they would prefer that we do not talk about how we experience working with people who are ill, may suffer, and will die. Perhaps they do not want to bear witness to this encounter, which reminds us of our own mortality and that of our loved ones. Indeed, we live in a dominant culture where the effects on the body and person of serious illness and dying are increasingly hidden from view, as is the distress and suffering that may accompany this (Lawton, 2000). Associated with these concealments is the idea that to live with a serious illness you are living in another world, separate and apart from the 'kingdom of the well' (Sontag, 1991, p. 3). And as professionals we hold temporary 'visas' into this world, and some of us are likely to have inhabited or to be inhabiting this world ourselves. So we view the question, 'How do you do what you do?' as an invitation for us to share some of our experiences of being in the 'world' of illness, what it is like for us to be with people who are seriously ill and will die, rather than to keep these experiences hidden and on the margins.

Throughout this chapter we will introduce you to some of the individuals, families and colleagues we have worked with and learned from, highlighting the tensions and dilemmas of our work as well as the possibilities and inspirational moments it creates through the people we meet. And so we invite you the reader to join us in this world.

We hope to show that while, in different ways, our professional training invites us to take up positions of 'knowing', in our experience this can prove to be inadequate in the face of death, dying and its associated threat of loss; not only in terms of being helpful to our patients/clients but also in terms of equipping ourselves for being with the grief and mourning we frequently experience in our professional lives. The reflections we include below are part of the story of how we have moved away from a knowing position, and how in so doing we hope to honour the humanity of those who seek our care. The cases we describe are real, but we have changed the names and some of the clinical details in order to protect the anonymity of those involved.

A psychologist's journey within the world of the seriously ill

On not assuming we know

I would like to share a memory with you of the first death I remember. At the time I was nine years old.

It was night and I was in my bed. My mum comes in and sits on my bed, she is close to me. I sit up. 'Your granddad died.' She falters, the room is dark, and she leans forward, shoulders pulled in, hands to her face, covering her face. I put my arm carefully around her. She is warm. Quiet tears. I am quiet; it is quiet. I want to be close to my mum. I am close to my mum.

A tenderness is shown between my mum and me, we are doing tenderness, our bodies move together and I respond to my mum's leaning forward. There is little talk. This memory resonates for me as it shows how as a young girl with little 'rational or practical knowing' my body instead responded to my mum's. I moved close to her and mirrored her physical movements. I was not limited or constrained by thinking that I might need or have to behave in a particular way, and I was able to be with my mum. Sometimes in our work we are unintentionally pulled away from being with people in the moment, as the following shows.

My psychology colleague, Susan Hennessey, and I began the process of creating the Psychology Support for Palliative Care service in the inner London borough of Tower Hamlets over four years ago. In our initial conversations Susan and I were excited at the possibilities this opportunity represented and yet also daunted at its seeming impossibility. We were both left wondering, 'What can we offer to people and families who might be in distress and suffering? What can we hope to offer to people who will die? And what do other professionals and commissioners expect from us?' We seemed very small in relation to what we imagined to be a profound life experience for those we would be meeting and intending to help. And so we began to read. We read personal accounts and stories from those living with and dying from a life-limiting condition (e.g. Diamond, 1998; Picardie, 1998) and theoretical accounts (e.g. Yalom, 2008; Bowlby, 1969, 1973, 1980). These stories 'filled us up', moved us to tears and inspired us, and yet the question remained, 'How can we help?' How can the theory and knowledge of psychology contribute and make a difference for those struggling towards the end of life?

Susan and I took a moment one day to reflect on how we had responded to our dilemma. We were amused at our tenacious 'over-reading', and yet curious as to its function and meaning. Reading has been an important part of our personal lives since childhood and, perhaps captivated by the richness that stories gave us, we both went on to study English as our first degrees. Stories I read connect with and inspire my imagination and learning, enrich my lived experience, and have helped influence and inform my clinical practice. They also represent a place of comfort and refuge, and offer protection at times when tensions and conflict may be impacting on me. I was reading others' stories and experiences of living with serious illness and theoretical accounts as a way to help me to understand and 'know how' to be with clients and create a service. I was looking to these books as I would a guide and manual; I was seeking a rational and practical 'knowing' in the belief that it would help both Susan and me know what to do and how to behave with individuals and families. In addition, as lead of our service, I was pulled by a dominant idea that commissioners and other healthcare professionals might be expecting us to be 'experts' and to show 'expertise', that is, that we 'hold' certain psychological theories and knowledge about illness, dying and bereavement that others do not, and these will guide what we do and how we respond. And perhaps I believed these meta-theories and knowledge would keep me safe – a protection from the distress and suffering I expected to witness (see Fredman, 1997).

The idea that we had to be 'expert' and that it is possible to know how a person who is dying is likely to feel, which then guides how we 'should' behave or act, rather than being helpful was diminishing and constraining. Noticing this was experienced like a large outward breath that created space to reposition ourselves from being outsiders 'looking in' and knowing how to view ourselves as participants of a process with the people we meet. It also helped us reconnect with our values and preferred ways of practising as clinical psychologists, where we 'join in' conversation with those seeking our help from a spirit of collaboration, curiosity and 'not knowing'; valuing the multiple experiences of those living with serious illness.

The individuals and families I meet are the experts on what it means to live with a life-limiting illness. They are the ones experiencing living with and dying from illness. I am not. The experience is also unique to them as a family and/or an individual; although there may be common elements in the dying process there is no single way to experience dying, despite guidelines and policies that may suggest otherwise. Some people will experience dying peacefully and for others it will be painful, distressing, awful (see Lawton, 2000). And as practitioners we bear witness to the range of these experiences. Within a changing and uncertain physical health context, therefore, a 'not knowing' position can help, as it shows we are willing to listen and learn from the people we meet; it means we meet families or individuals where they are and can travel with them. And it creates a context of safety, of being safe with uncertainty. A 'not-knowing' approach does not mean I do not hold expertise, but rather that I can use my expertise to *join with* people in conversation, and closely follow their feedback and use their language. I am interested and curious in what people are saying and so the process is the outcome, as together new meanings, stories and action are created (Anderson and Goolishian, 1992). They are the stories not yet told.

Keeping in time: Kate and Hal

Kate lived with her partner, Hal. Both were in their late forties. She had a diagnosis of lung cancer and metastatic brain cancer. The clinical nurse specialist (CNS), who was part of the Community Palliative Care Team (CPCT), was keen for her to engage with the support she and her team could offer Kate and her family at home. However, both Kate and Hal believed the cancer could be cured through lifestyle and the Gersen diet (an organic, non-chemical 'treatment' for cancer). The CNS found it difficult to accommodate the family's views and so sought psychological help.

I encourage my colleagues to talk with me about people they are intending to refer, when this is possible. In such a conversation I will typically ask relationally focused questions: 'Who is this concern a problem for?' and 'Whose idea is it that help is needed?' And so I am not locating the problem within Kate and Hal or my colleague, but rather I am viewing the problem in relationship with people and checking out who is most and least affected or concerned, which helps me consider whom it might be best to meet or help (see Fredman, 1997). The CNS told me that she just 'didn't get' Kate's and Hal's belief that her cancer could be cured, and experienced frustration at their 'denial of reality'. The situation left her feeling helpless and exasperated and to manage the dilemma she invited me to help Kate and Hal.

We can be pulled by the context of time in our work with people who are living with a life-limiting illness, particularly in relation to the knowledge we may hold in relation to a person's diagnosis and prognosis, and our experience of supporting others with similar diagnoses. Given the CNS's wealth of experience supporting people with lung cancer and brain metastases, and knowing its likely effects on the body, she had a strong desire to be of help to the couple, to comfort and soothe them with nursing care 'before it was too late'. She felt terribly stuck and confused when her ideas and theories about what could help did not fit for Kate and Hal. This temporal confusion creates a tension and dilemma for the CNS as the dominant professional context informing her practice is challenged, which then paralyses what she can say or do.

The CNS may have felt anxious that Kate would experience a distressing death due to her belief that the cancer could be cured, and felt powerless to help from the medical position she was acting out of, where the reality was that Kate would die. And staying in a medical context of what will help, meant the CNS was perhaps also protecting herself from considering her personal beliefs and meanings about death and evaluating these against those held by the couple (Fredman, 1997, p. 13). For example, she may have used her personal experiences of faith to help her consider the faith in the Gersen diet that Hal and Kate held. Withdrawing and seeking my help therefore might help protect the CNS both from experiencing the dilemmas and pain the couple were likely to be experiencing following Kate's diagnosis, and the tension this created for her as a nurse.

Joining together in helping relationships

The CNS and I agreed it might be useful for us to meet with Kate and Hal together, with the intention that I would facilitate a conversation between them. Inviting the CNS, I hoped, would help establish her connection with Kate and Hal and enhance their relationship, showing also that we could work together creatively. Hal decided he did not want to join us at this meeting, and so Kate, the CNS and I met. To connect collaboratively with Kate, and Kate with the CNS, I remained curious about Kate's life and what was important for her at this moment. I asked Kate, 'What are the ideas you had about our meeting today?' 'What are your main concerns?' 'Are these concerns the same as Hal's or different?' 'How do you view the CNS's support/help right now?' and 'What would you most like from her at this point in time?' These kinds of questions created space and privilege for Kate's concerns, and also created a relational focus: for example, I asked Kate to consider Hal's perspective, although he was not physically present, and we talked about what the relationship between Kate and the CNS might look like. And so the CNS was invited to hear Kate and meaningfully respond to her hopes. This gave permission for the CNS to say what she could and could not do, opened up possibilities rather than closed them down, helped the CNS and Kate collaboratively decide how they could best 'work together', and identified other resources in Kate's circle of support.

I met Kate weekly in her housing association terraced house; often there were many people coming and going, while their dog scampered around and the proud white cat perched above Kate on the comfy, dishevelled sofa. Hal would keep himself busy in the background, making healthy food, smoothies and snacks for Kate, or chopping wood in their back yard. I got to know Kate's close friend, her mum and son, all of whom took part in our conversations at some point, when Kate felt it could be helpful. I would make a point of informally 'checking in' with Hal as I came and left their house, respecting that for the moment this was his preferred way of being with me and with Kate's illness.

One day Kate told me she was scared; she had noticed changes in her body. I had noticed changes too: a tired body drifting in and out of sleep, a persistent dry cough, a slurring of speech. She cried, slow tears. Being with her in this moment was both painful and sad; it was visceral and was experienced through our bodies. My heart moved in response to her tears; my heart went out to hers. This bodily connection helped me begin to name our shared experience. I proceeded tentatively, seeking her permission regarding what might or might not be OK to ask, and establishing in advance things that might be difficult for her to hear: 'Is it OK for me to ask a bit more about the changes you've noticed?' 'How would you like me to be with you?' 'This may be difficult . . .' 'I might have got this wrong . . .' Kate was no longer sure she could be cured, but did not want to 'give up' on the idea. She talked about wanting to know about chemical forms of pain relief and her fears regarding this in relation to side effects. She also wanted to protect Hal from her knowing about her changing physical health, and was unsure if she wanted to talk about the cancer.

Open acknowledgement that the cancer would not be cured perhaps challenged Kate's and Hal's identity and the relationship between them – one that placed value on living a toxin- and chemical-free lifestyle, and the values she held dear and that connected with her selfhood and integrity as a person. Giving up on this idea might be experienced therefore as a threat to, and potential loss of, the integrity of her self, and the relationships that mattered to her. Rather than seeing the contradictions Kate showed as a problem, I instead wanted to respect and acknowledge them – with regard to how she viewed herself in relation to Hal, and in relation with her self, the meaning of living, being in control and hope.

As Kate became increasingly unwell, I experienced a dilemma between wanting to join with her in relation to meaning and understanding, and taking a not-knowing position, and my professional duties and obligations towards her and Hal. Primarily I was concerned that the family did not know of the help available to them if she experienced acute physical pain and distress and as a consequence might call 999. I hypothesized that an emergency call-out and Kate's potential admission to hospital would not fit with the values they shared, that is, a preference for non-medical interventions. I had temporarily suspended this idea for a few weeks, until now, when I hoped it could be useful and timely, given her changing physical health. In view of these considerations, I decided to be transparent with Kate about my dilemma. I clarified with her my professional concerns: 'Kate, I'm holding a dilemma as a professional involved in supporting you – would it be OK to share this with you . . . what are your thoughts, do you have similar/different concerns?' By remaining transparent and clearly communicating to Kate my professional duty and associated concerns, it was possible to remain ethical and respectful towards her. And it gave us a way to proceed *together*.

Kate died at home a few weeks later. She and I wrote a letter together for Hal, which Kate wanted me to give to him after her funeral. She wrote a will. Her friends and family continued to remain a large presence, and Kate orchestrated their comings and goings; this was important, as it was associated with her position as head of the household. She and Hal remained closely involved in decisions regarding medical pain relief. Kate's friend and Hal organized a funeral that combined both Christian and pagan ideas to accommodate the many different views and beliefs about living, dying and mourning that Kate, her friends and family held.

Ritual, memory and mourning: making sense of the work I do

I visit most people in their homes, and for almost all I become a regular visitor until someone dies. I have been genuinely moved by people's acceptance at allowing me to enter their worlds, albeit this is only a brief encounter. And in my hope to be of help and influence to them, they too influence me. I have been humbled by the people and families I have met in my work, all of whom have enabled me to learn and grow both professionally and personally. The connection with people and families who are experiencing serious illness and dying has affected most aspects of my life. I value being in the moment a lot more and have made some important life decisions, such as leaving an unhappy relationship. My relationships with close family, friends and with my new partner and daughter have been enhanced and strengthened. Being in the world of the seriously ill is sometimes exhausting and terribly sad; people's stories, as we have noted, can 'fill you up'. And yet primarily my work shows me the value and meaning of our connections with others, and thus enriches and expands my lived experience.

Sometimes I do not have the opportunity to mark an ending with the people I have been closely connected with in my practice, particularly if they die unexpectedly, or if they have not wanted to leave the world of the living, which makes it terribly hard and/or untimely to talk about 'letting go' before they die. These experiences can leave me feeling emotionally 'adrift', and so, adapting an idea from narrative therapy (see White, 2007), I have developed a ritual of writing a goodbye letter to the deceased which I keep in my clinical notes. The letter tells the story of our therapeutic encounter and marks the person's resources, what we struggled with together, what I appreciated about the person and found inspirational, and how these memories will inform me both professionally and personally. This letter is not intended to be sent but helps me to make sense of my loss, commemorates our connection and honours the memory of our relationship.

Creating space at work with others to consider the effects of the experiences I encounter is also invaluable. My colleague, Susan, and I make regular space with one another to share the memories of those we have met in our work, our struggles and our joys, and the meaning for us when someone we have been connected with through our work dies. Our memory of the times we have shared with individuals and families lives on. Sharing these memories enables us to create meaning through our experiences of loss, and as a mourning ritual connects with future possibilities, informing both our clinical practice and our service development.

I believe that a not-knowing approach helps me to connect with others in a meaningful way and to do the work that I do. Hearing the voices of those living with, and dying from, a serious illness, centralizing their concerns, and viewing the multiple contexts and relationships within which an individual lives and is connected, is, I believe, at the heart of a respectful, flexible, ethical and creative practice. The perspective also allows me to make sense of the effects of loss and mourning from both a professional and personal point of view.

A doctor's journey

Medical training: immunity from dying

From the very early days of my undergraduate training in medicine I have been taught to know what to do about the problems patients face, but at the same time, subtly and unconsciously, to understand myself to be separate from those others whom we term 'patients'.

My first exposure to death 'in the flesh' came a few weeks into my first term at medical school. At 19 I was a little older than many of my fellow students and was not among the one or two who, that first time, could not manage to stay in the anatomy room (later, a few students would faint at their first experience of being in an operating theatre – something it took them a long time to live down). I remember a high level of anxiety as we waited outside the room to 'meet' the body of the person who was to be dissected by us, piece by piece, over the next two years.

But what needs to happen deep inside someone's head for them to be able to take a knife and cut through the flesh of another person, albeit a dead one? And to go on doing that, day after day for many months, slowly taking the body apart? My sense now is that, in order to be able to do so, it helped me to see the body as somehow 'other', as having very little to do with me, as an object rather than a fellow person. At the time we didn't notice this 'otherness' being instilled within us and we certainly failed to recognize how this process might impact on our future ability to maintain a sense of the personhood of those who would be our patients in years to come. There was no preparation from our teachers, no discussion among ourselves, no internal reflection – we simply didn't have the language to begin to describe an experience that was literally dehumanizing. And we certainly had no interest in who this person, this body, had been: what the person's life story was; what his or her interests and memories and connections in the world were. Nothing, it was just a body. Instead there was a sense that being able to cope – more than that, being unaffected by our experiences in the anatomy room – was an important preparation for our future careers, a key component of becoming socialized into the medical elite. So I was just happy not to have left the room, not to have been a 'fainter', to have passed the test, to have shown myself to be in some small way invincible and increasingly different from the uninitiated lay public, from whom I would now be for ever separate. A similar but much harder test of my training in separateness and in 'being unaffected' was to come a few years later, when I had to cut a skin sample from the body of a perfect, beautiful, but stillborn little girl.

My training was teaching me to be an observer rather than a participant, as if the fate that had overtaken the person whose body I had been cutting up was one that would never befall me. But I was also being taught a second and powerful message about the weakness of showing emotion; about the vulnerability you would be exposed to if you allowed yourself to feel.

As my training progressed I learned how to identify and treat the multitude of possible diseases and traumas that I would see during my working life. Of course, as a doctor it is frequently important that I do know how to do these things, but at the same time there was no acknowledgement that sometimes this approach would fail; no sense that this way of knowing had its limitations, let alone how to recognize when these had been reached. Because the reality is, of course, that I was not unaffected by these traumatizing experiences; I only told myself I was. And nor was I separate, as if made of an immune and immortal material. I am not suggesting that all, or even most, doctors respond as I did, and there is nothing unusual about a newly qualified doctor frequently being exposed to patients' deaths, but perhaps these were necessary self-deceptions, being, as I then was, so poorly equipped to deal with dying and death. How else are doctors supposed to cope with a life working at the edges of existence? How else might someone in their early twenties be able to take a scalpel to a dead baby's body one minute and, without pause, walk into the room of a mother in labour the next? How else are doctors to 'know' and to 'do' in the face of suffering, except by being someone who cannot themselves suffer?

The question is, then: What price is paid in order to maintain within oneself an illusion of invincibility? Looking back now I cannot believe that I didn't grieve for that baby somehow, but I also know that I had been taught no ways of sharing my experiences with my community, no ways of allowing myself to feel appropriately sad about her, and I cannot tell you where my grief for her has gone.

Dying as defeat

In practice, the vast majority of doctors are not unfeeling or uncaring individuals, despite aspects of our training, and yet I wonder to what extent those early anatomy-room experiences remain somewhere within doctors and colour our approaches to death, dying and grief; aspects of living that are clear challenges to the medical model of 'knowing' because ultimately we are unable to prevent death (the death rate is, after all, 100 per cent), nor do we know what it is to be dead.

I met Ruth when I was a junior doctor in paediatrics. She was 14 years old, but looked much younger, her body stunted by cystic fibrosis and bloated by steroids. To me she looked like a Buddha, sitting on her bed, but she acted much more like a prima donna: she was a feisty girl who hated hospital and disliked most of her doctors and nurses, or at least disliked what they did to her. She took an intense interest in the medical chart that was always attached to the foot of her bed and for some reason this intimidated me. Shortly after she was admitted to the ward I was tasked with taking her blood for some tests, something I was told she would actively resist. I approached her with trepidation, introduced myself and sat with her for a while. I explained what I had to do and, as anticipated, was met with a complete refusal. In a moment of desperation I picked up her cuddly toy; she would allow me to take her blood, I told her, or the elephant would 'get it'. She laughed, held out her arm and I took the sample.

We were friends after that, and I spent as much time as I could with her each day. She even gave me the gift of allowing me to suction her tracheostomy (a surgical hole in her windpipe just above her sternum through which she breathed and due to which she had little speech), something very few had the privilege to do and a procedure that, as with so much in medicine, was oddly intimate. I no longer saw her as an irritatingly unhelpful patient (Don't patients understand I am there to help them? Don't they know they should be grateful?), but instead came to recognize the young person striving against the odds to develop towards adulthood; someone with very little control over what happened to her.

In the end the odds were indeed stacked far too greatly against her, and as her lungs deteriorated she became less well. She lost her feistiness; her face showed a desperate vulnerability and she became fearful. They (I don't know who) took away her medical chart. As the most junior member of the team I was shielded from her dying by my consultant, but I was very aware that he and the senior nursing staff were spending more and more time with Ruth and her parents behind a closed door. She died not very long after that. The professionals quietly left her room, exhausted, defeated and in something of a state of shock. The death had been traumatic. I got on with my work, not knowing what else to do.

I think of Ruth quite often, even 20 years later. With my current experiences in palliative care I question what it meant to her to have her chart removed. Was that helpful for her, or did the adults think that it was a way of protecting a child? Did anyone ask her? I wonder what opportunities there were for her to ask for the truth and, in a way appropriate to her age and capability, to be given it. What preparations for death might be right for a child of 14 to undertake, if any? What chance was she offered to do so? I suspect I know the answers to these questions because I think that the doctors and nurses, even with Ruth's well-being uppermost in their thinking, did not know how to make sense of her dying themselves, and so certainly did not know how to help her to do so. How do doctors square the circle that, on the one hand, tells us that patients are not us, that we should know how to make every-thing better, that death is the enemy and, on the other, that this girl was in a distress that they could not begin to deal with, that she was going to die whatever they did? I was later to discover that it takes a willingness to accept that your lot is the same as your patient's in order to begin to be able to listen to him or her. In this case, Ruth's death and its effect on the staff, myself included, were not addressed. It was almost as if she hadn't existed in our lives.

On not getting better

The concept of 'getting better' is an odd one, given that the population of patients with whom I work are those with far advanced life-limiting illnesses. And yet I, in common with almost all the healthcare staff I know, need something to 'get better' for the patient, in order to believe that we are fulfilling our purpose in the face of dying, death and bereave-ment. One of my most challenging patients, therefore, was Sarah, a lady in her late sixties who had been diagnosed with a progressing cancer and who, no matter what I did, only ever got worse.

Her story is difficult to encapsulate but is one of terrible suffering and a death that was far from 'good'. It seems to me now, with the benefit of hindsight, that she occupied a position of wanting to be treated – initially for the cancer itself, later for the terrible pain she experienced – and at the same time not trusting that anything could, or perhaps should, help her. But at the time I had not come to this view, rather I could only focus on what interventions – medical, social, psychological, spiritual – I and my colleagues could make in order to take away her pain. However, my training had not prepared me for my – indeed, our collective – impotence in the face of the extremity of her suffering: she would spend all day unable to get out of bed, due to the terrible pain that originated in her back and extended down one leg. Over time this leg became weaker and atrophied compared to the other leg. I, along with my CNS colleague, tried every trick we knew to try to reduce her pain. On almost every occasion a new medication would initially appear to be successful, only to fail within two or three doses; more than that, each new medication seemed to Sarah to increase her pain. I sought a second opinion and transferred her to a tertiary cancer unit where she was given an injection directly into the spine (similar to the epidurals used for pain relief during labour), but again this approach merely served to increase the pain.

So it was something of an odd relief to me when I finally ran out of ideas and I could stop 'knowing'. I felt that I could stop subjecting her to futile interventions and instead try simply to be with her. I realized that I had been carrying a sense that I was somehow making her a victim of my need to reduce her pain – even though this was what she wanted and she had gone along with all my suggestions. Now, however, I had nothing more to offer and instead, with help, I relearned what I had left to give when I had no more to give from my knowledge and experience. And so I would visit every week, offer nothing but instead sit with her for a while, try to be genuinely attentive to what she was experiencing – in this sense, to 'not know' so that I could learn something new – and to acknowledge the horror of her suffering. I did not find this easy, but every week she would ask me to return.

This story does not have a happy ending; I did indeed bear witness to her suffering, but it was not enough, although for a time perhaps she found solace in being heard. In the end she had a distressing, uncomfortable and ultimately sedated death. This was difficult not only for her, but also for her family and for the hospice staff who, like me, struggled with having 'nothing' to offer.

Reflecting on my experience of working with Sarah, now that some time has passed, I recognize the dilemma I was facing: what is the correct, ethical way to combine the two approaches of knowing and not knowing? And for whose benefit do I occupy each of these two positions? I also realize that I have not felt the same weight of unexpressed grief for Sarah as I did for Ruth, despite the level of my involvement and the similarly traumatic nature of their dyings. Perhaps this reflects a different level of connection with Sarah than with Ruth; perhaps it is just because I am older and more experienced now; but perhaps it is because, in living with the tension between knowing and not knowing, I have found an approach that allows me both to practise in my professional capacity and to satisfy the need to relate honestly to my patients as fellow humans walking a similar journey. Perhaps the imperfections with which I necessarily do both are part of that same story.

A reflection by Sue

I have frequently heard expressed this sense of frustration and helplessness, when a medical consultant is faced with the dilemma of being medically responsible for someone who does not seem to be soothed physically or emotionally by the consultant's interventions. Here the very help, knowledge and information that Jon hopes to offer (different forms of pain relief), which is consistent with his ethics of practice and that he believes will be of benefit, is apparently unhelpful. And so his professional identity is challenged and he continues to seek alternative forms of pain relief until the options run out (see Fredman, Johnson and Petronic, 2010). This could create a position of opposition, where the medical team's version of what will help creates a physical and emotional distance between the patient and the medical team, and prevents collaboration. And thus 'being with Sarah' is experienced as 'doing nothing'. Jon's responses here may be understood from the interconnecting contexts of his medical profession and the nomenclature of palliative care advocating a 'good death' for all (e.g. DoH, 2008).

It is tough for medical consultants who, along with nurses, are often the key professionals involved in engaging and maintaining individuals' and families' relationships with healthcare systems at the end of a person's life. Within this role they may assume sole responsibility for creating the conditions for a 'good death' and getting the dying 'right'. A distressing death therefore may be experienced as failure, and the practitioners may feel that the best medical care has not been provided. This may lead them to feel exposed and under scrutiny, with the effect that they experience vulnerability as practitioners. Of course, to have our professional help rejected or dismissed and described as unhelpful can also have a significant emotional effect on us, as it is likely to connect and resonate with our personal experiences of rejection, and our reasons for being in a caring profession, particularly with those who are dying, and wanting to help others.

Once our options regarding what we believe will help are exhausted, the continued experience of extreme distress and suffering can lead us to withdraw from, abandon or ignore a person, as it creates a tension within the context of our professional knowing. At times of extreme distress and suffering, being with a person – metaphorically holding on – can show the person that neither she nor the professional involved have failed. Rather than abandoning Sarah in her distress and suffering, Jon compassionately joined her in this world. This can then further create possibilities for us to be with people in these moments where we move from a professional context of help to draw upon the many other resources and contexts available to us, for example as friends, parents, our age or gender, and which might help us to understand and connect with distress and suffering and enable us to be meaningfully with those we intend to help.

We are participants in the dying process

We do not want to suggest that knowing how and knowing what cannot be useful in working with people who are dying and those close to them. However, if our intention is to behave ethically and respectfully in relation to people and their bodies, we need to ask permission from those we hope to engage as to whether our knowledge – about how bodies respond to an illness and the dying process, use of pain medication and so on – might be of help to them. We also need to inform them of the duties and obligations we might be bound by, such as the requirement on us to assess capacity or risk (see Fredman, Johnson and Petronic, 2010). Asserting our own agenda without permission stops us respectfully listening, hearing and being in a relationship with people, families, colleagues, and can silence those we want to help or result in their withdrawal and disengagement. It can also mean we withdraw and disengage. By acknowledging the limits of a professionalized approach to dying, we begin to see our patients/clients as people just like us; far from being 'too close to home', perhaps this is paradoxically a key to managing successfully our own grief reactions as professionals, as it helps us begin to make sense of the many ways people experience dying and death.

We hope in this chapter to have shared with you an idea that being with people in the moment and taking a not-knowing approach helps create meaningful, wise and thoughtful connections. Such bonds are formed with both the individuals and families we meet and our colleagues. This approach enriches our practice as it helps us appreciate and value the range of resources and experiences we all hold and that can help us do the work we do. We hope, too, to have given our answer to the question, 'How do you do what you do?' Being with people who are dying is not necessarily gloomy or depressing; it is instead rich and varied. Like the people we meet in our daily practice, we too are moved by the experience, and appropriately so.

Appendix – Writing this chapter

During the process of writing this chapter with my colleague and ally Jon, I read a wonderful book called *Being with Older People*. In this the authors describe the process they used to create the book (Fredman, Anderson and Stott, 2010, pp. 1–29). They shared memories with one another, a first-person account of both professional practice and personal experiences of being with older people, a story-telling through which they generated themes and connections, and noticed similarities and differences between their experiences. The telling and retelling of their experiences shaped the book's themes and content. I was greatly influenced by this process, as the authors show how through connecting with memories and talking of these in the first person, uninhibited by theory or thinking, a visceral range of new connections is made, and by joining together in conversation, new ways of seeing, experiencing, feeling and new possibilities are created. The process and method also positions professionals as active participants engaged *within*, and affected and influenced – both personally and professionally – by the people we meet in our daily work, rather than as distant and objective bystanders removed from the lives and experiences of those we meet and intend to help.

The process of writing described by these authors (Fredman, Anderson and Stott, 2010) gave a name to how Jon and I had decided to write this chapter, albeit a bit 'looser' in process and method. We met and joined in conversation over a number of weeks, and reflected upon our experiences as a psychologist and medical consultant working in palliative care: what this means for us, how our professional identities inform our practice and how we experience our working relationship. Together we shared memories of some of the people and families we have met and the colleagues we work alongside. We invited into this space the 'ghosts' of our past, the memory of those who have died and their significant others, the individuals and families who had touched and moved us and who deeply affected, challenged and inspired us both personally and professionally. We reflected that these 'ghosts of the past' are perhaps also part of the organizational memory within which we work, and that their stories go on to influence how an organization understands, experiences and responds to those who are ill and will die. And so we are all affected by those we meet in our work, at both an individual and a wider professional and organizational level.

References

Anderson, A. and Goolishian, Harold (1992), 'The Client is the Expert: A Not-Knowing Approach to Therapy', in McNamee, Sheila and Gergen, Kenneth J., *Therapy as Social Construction*, London: Sage.

Bowlby, J. (1969), *Attachment. Attachment and Loss*, vol. 1, 2nd edn, New York: Basic Books.

Bowlby, J. (1973), *Separation: Anxiety and Anger. Attachment and Loss*, vol. 2, London: Hogarth Press.

Bowlby, J. (1980), *Loss: Sadness and Depression. Attachment and Loss*, vol. 3, London: Hogarth Press.

Department of Health (2008), *End of Life Care Strategy*, London: Department of Health.

Diamond, J. (1998), *Because Cowards Get Cancer Too*, London: Vermilion.

Frank, A. W. (1995), *The Wounded Storyteller: Body, Illness and Ethics*, Chicago: University of Chicago Press.

Fredman, Glenda (1997), *Death Talk: Conversations with Children and Families*, London: Karnac.

Fredman, G., Anderson, E. and Stott, J., eds (2010), *Being With Older People: A Systemic Approach*, London: Karnac.

Fredman, G., Johnson, S. and Petronic, G. (2010), 'Sustaining the Ethics of Systemic Practice in Contexts of Risk and Diagnosis', in Fredman, G., Anderson, E. and Stott, J., eds, *Being With Older People: A Systemic Approach*, London: Karnac.

Lang, P., Little, M. and Cronen, V. E. (1990), 'The Systemic Professional Domains of Action and the Question of Neutrality', *Human Systems: The Journal of Systemic Consultation and Management*, 1(1): 32–46.

Lawton, J. (2000), *The Dying Process: Patients' Experience of Palliative Care*, London: Routledge.

Picardie, R. (1998), *Before I Say Goodbye*, London: Penguin.

Riikonen, E. (1999), 'Inspiring Dialogues and Relational Responsibility', in McNamee, S. and Gergen, K. J., eds, *Relational Responsibility: Resources for Sustainable Dialogue*, London: Sage.

Shotter, J. (1993), *Conversational Realities: Constructing Life through Language*, London: Sage.

Smith, S. and Hennessey, S. (2009), 'Community Teams' Views of Psychology Support Within Palliative Care', unpublished.

Sontag, S. (1991), *Illness as Metaphor and AIDS and its Metaphors*, London: Penguin.

White, M. (2007), *Maps of Narrative Practice*, New York: W. W. Norton.

Yalom, I. (2008), *Staring at the Sun: Overcoming the Dread of Death*, London: Piatkus.

6

Reflections on Jewish approaches to death, grief and mourning

———————

HOWARD COOPER

Living in this world

It's not that I'm afraid to die. I just don't want to be there when it happens.

(Woody Allen)

An imam, a vicar and a rabbi are travelling together in a car. The car crashes and, sadly, they are all killed. Their souls ascend to heaven – where else? – where they are met by St Peter, who says to them: 'If you look down from here you can see your bodies being laid out in your coffins and caskets ready for your funerals; and your family, friends and congregants are gathering round, mourning over you. My question to each of you is: "What would you like to hear them say?"' The imam says: 'I would like to hear them say I was a wonderful husband, a fine spiritual leader and a caring human being.' The vicar says: 'I'd like to hear that I was a wonderful teacher, and a servant of God who made a huge difference to people's lives.' St Peter turns to the rabbi: 'And you, rabbi, what would you like to hear them say?' And the rabbi replies: 'Oh, I'd like to hear them say – "Look, he's moving!"'

I first heard that joke from one of my teachers, Rabbi Lionel Blue. And if I start my reflections on Jewish approaches to death, grief and mourning with a less than serious observation, it is because one of the things I learned from Lionel is that from a Jewish perspective there is no situation we face as human beings that cannot lend itself to humour. For humour – although it can be used defensively or aggressively as a way of protecting ourselves from painful feelings – is a hallmark of our humanity. Laughter can be life-enhancing, life-affirming and, perhaps because Jewish life has historically and collectively known its fair share of suffering, there is a determined emphasis within Judaic tradition and culture not to let sadness have the last word. Humour does not protect us from the reality of grief and loss – but it does offer another perspective, a larger vision: it reminds us of the boundlessness of life, and our capacity to be delighted, surprised, entertained and sometimes inspired by the serendipitous and idiosyncratic nature of life in this world.

Traditionally – as this joke intuits – Jews focus on this world, living in this world with as much liveliness and integrity and mindfulness and compassion as we can muster; and there is relatively little speculation about the next world, or 'heaven'. Although there are strands of Jewish thought that suggest that all of life is in a sense a preparation for death – 'This world is like a corridor to the world to come. Prepare yourself in the corridor so that you may enter the inner chamber,' says Rabbi Jacob (second century CE) in the Talmud – we are very much a this-worldly religion. The emotional and practical emphasis is on the here and now, with that distinctive combination of down-to-earth ethical and ritual behaviour that the conscientious Jew weaves together in daily life: food laws, charitable giving, Sabbath observance, interpersonal behaviour, concern for the well-being of one's family, community, neighbours, planet, business ethics, life-cycle celebrations . . . it is a 'hands-on' religion focused on the spirituality of everyday life. And one of the things that this attentiveness to the practicalities of daily life means is that we take the reality of death (and grief, and loss) seriously as an inevitable part of *this life* that has to be faced fully.

Indeed, there are ways in which Judaic thought nudges us towards seeing death as co-extensive with life, as if time itself – chronological time – is partially an illusion: a Hasidic saying has it that 'People are always passing through two doors, out of this world and into the next, and out and in again.' This thought is reflected too in the words of the Israeli poet Lea Goldberg (1911–70), who articulates it with a delicate and profound simplicity:

> The eighth part (at least) of everything
> is death. Its weight is not great.
> How lightly and with what casual grace
> we carry it with us everywhere we go.
> On fresh awakenings, on journeys,
> or in lovers' talk – though seemingly
> left behind in some dark corner –
> it is always with us. Weighing
> hardly anything at all.

When life meets death

For everything there is a season, and a time to every purpose under heaven: a time for birth, and a time for death.
(Ecclesiastes 3.1–2)

In the early years of my professional working life, when I was employed as a rabbi in a large suburban community, my days were filled with frenetic activity. An endless round of meetings, pastoral visits, sermon writing, report writing, phone calls, administration. And then in the evening I would often have to go to a stranger's house to lead prayers: a house of mourning where a family was 'sitting *shiva*' after the death of a relative.

Later on in this chapter I will outline some of the specific rites and rituals that Judaism prescribes around death and the period after it, but I am starting with a more subjective description because I want to convey the felt experience of death within the Jewish community, as well as illustrating the gap that often now exists between inherited ancestral traditions and the complex emotional reality of people's lives.

As I made my way to the mourner's house I would reflect on the many mixed and powerful emotions I might meet there; how as a rabbi I would be called upon to relate to all the sadness, the pain and the grief that the event had generated; or perhaps the emotion would be relief – and the guilt about the relief. There'd be memories and stories – sometimes loving, sometimes bitter – of what had been shared and what had been said; and what had never been shared and what had never been spoken, missed opportunities. Sometimes I knew there would be distressed or angry questions about life's meaning, and God's purpose, and the brutality of endings, and the unfairness and burden of lives lived without certainty or clarity about what it's all about – years spent working for security, for dignity, and it comes to this: the grave, the shroud, and our little lives rounded with a sleep. At other times there would be tearful but resigned acceptance that an earthly life had now ended. Or perhaps there'd be a rather distressing (to me) absence of feelings, and in their place a rather brittle chirpiness and a sense, articulated or not, that tears on this sad occasion were a sign of weakness, or even rather infra dig.

So I would drive through the darkness holding in mind these thoughts, preparing myself for an encounter with the often unarticulated demandingness of the mourners: their pain and sorrow and, particularly if the death had been unexpected, their need to make sense of what had happened. Their questions – our questions – are not of course new ones: 'What does a person gain for all the toil they have expended?' (Ecclesiastes 3.9). Many Jews, now quite unversed in the texts of their tradition, are still asking the old, eternal questions.

In my mind's eye, these drives to *shiva* homes always take place accompanied by rain or fog or snow. Cocooned in my car I would appreciate the womb-like security of the vehicle's warmth and silence. Sometimes though, as distractions from (preparations for?) the uncertainties ahead, I would listen to my favourite tracks: the Beatles, Bob Dylan, Bruce Springsteen, Jefferson Airplane. (This dates me.) And I would wonder if I should be listening to this on my way to a *shiva*. Wouldn't late Beethoven be a more suitable preparation? Apparently not.

It's been a long day. I've worked hard. I'm feeling exhausted. Empty. I have nothing left to give. Enough, already. 'God, this is your work . . . I don't need it, don't want it . . . If you want me to do it you'll have to give me something . . . because I've got nothing . . .' This is not my theology. It's the regressed meanderings of a tired man. Otherwise known as prayer. A prayer from a rabbi who doesn't believe in that kind of prayer.

I arrive at the house. I get out of the car. All I know is: 'You will be given what you need.' Which is what happens. Not every time, but often enough to know that wherever it comes from – whether it is an inner resource or an outer gift – some animating energy enables us to be with what unfolds, moment by moment. What I experience (from time to time) in the house of mourning is something at work within us, between us, around us, which the wisdom of old called by a myriad names. The Psalmist captured this spirit at the end of Psalm 90: 'May the favour of the Eternal be upon us: to support us in the work we do, and support the work we do.' These words – part of the funeral service – are both a plea and a celebration. Set against our helplessness, there is the hope (and promise) that something holds us through our life, as we live and as we face death.

And so, in the house of mourning the words of prayer are spoken. And space is created for people to share their memories, eloquently or disjointedly, as the deceased is evoked once more. And there are tears. And there is silence. And a kind of catharsis occurs. Amid the disquiet of grief there is stillness and there are moments of eternity. Life facing death. Then there is release, and the beginning of renewal for those who mourn. Something is working its way through. And suddenly we are back into the world: the cups of tea, the edgy bonhomie, the gossip and the garrulousness, the workaday concerns, the abundance and super-fluity of everyday life, more life, triumphing over the fact of death. Almost as if the deceased had never been – though none of us believes that.

As I leave and set off for home – or the next meeting – I recall the memorial words I have just spoken: 'Everlasting God, help us to realize more and more that time and space are not the measure of all things. Though our eyes do not see, teach us to understand that the soul of our dear one is not cut off. Love does not die, and truth is stronger than the grave.' And even for contemporary Jews, many of whom doubt the existence of an 'everlasting God' and are baffled by the notion of a 'soul', even for those very many secular-minded Jews who have banished religious belief from their lives, I know that these words, uttered with quiet conviction in the presence of death and in the presence of those who mourn, I know that these words have – at least for a moment – pierced the layers of doubt, or indifference, or devout antagonism with which we as a community protect ourselves. Even if the talk after the prayers is of football or fashion or finance, in the *shiva* house we have, in spite of it all, seen into the truth of things. For as the anonymous biblical poet knew: life is precious, but death will come to us all. Each has its season. And we are left to con-template how soon it may be until the season changes for us.

Death and its rituals

The Eternal has given, and the Eternal has taken away:
may the name of the Eternal be blessed.
(Jewish funeral service, 2009, quoting from Job 1.21)

Contemporary Anglo-Jewry is a heterogeneous mix. There is a vibrant and growing Orthodox sector, for whom the rituals and practices of old are a default setting for unchanging religious practice; for these traditionalists, strict adherence to the fine

detail of *halacha* (religious law) is felt to be an essential affirmation of Jewish faith and identity.

There are many other Jews, members of non-Orthodox
communities, who will not follow all the traditions but adopt
a looser, more 'pic'n'mix' approach to ritual and tradition:
the emotional ties to traditional ways are still there, in varying
degrees of strength, yet modernity has pressed in upon them to
such an extent that there is an innate tension between religious
practices that could have been inherited from parents (or be a
distant memory from grandparents) and contemporary British
mores where religious affirmation might be acknowledged but
doesn't form the major part of a person's sense of self. Following
a death, many of these synagogue-affiliated Jews will want to
'do the right thing' in relation to the deceased – but may have
only the haziest notion as to what that involves.

And then there are the 25 per cent of UK Jews who are not
members of a synagogue and yet may feel themselves to be
Jewish in quite secular or cultural ways: smoked-salmon-and-
bagel Jews who create their own anthology of habits that keep
their Jewish identity from disappearing. And many of these –
though by no means all – are younger Jews who consciously
reject the sometimes narrow particularism of the mainstream
Jewish community in favour of a more universalistic Jewishness
committed to a variety of social, political or cultural causes
informed by the ancient spirit of Jewish ethical concern, but
now freed from the inherited insularity of previous generations.
This techno-savvy, switched-on e-generation still faces the question of how to mourn 'Jewishly' – but, freed from the strictures
of old about what 'must' be done, may yet find new and creative
ways of saying farewell to loved ones and managing the feelings
that are generated by this universal experience, death.

So – as this somewhat broad-brush portrait might suggest –
it is very hard to generalize about 'Jewish' approaches to death,
mourning and loss. Because every Jew has his or her own
individual connection to tradition, what applies to one person

may not apply for another. What Jews hold dear in relation to rituals or beliefs will not be the same from family to family. Or even within one family. Siblings may disagree with one another or with a surviving parent. When this is the case, emotions can run high in regard to the time-honoured practices surrounding death and its aftermath. This is not just a question of Jews being notoriously argumentative – we have a saying, 'two Jews, three opinions' – it is about how Jews today have very complicated, and confused, relationships to their inherited religious traditions.

Nevertheless, the experience of death and bereavement forces Jewish people into an encounter with hallowed traditions and beliefs laid down by their ancestors. And if one's relationship to Judaism is problematic or disputatious – as it is for so many contemporary Jews – this can lead to guilt. It's as if we are letting the side down if we depart too far from culturally sanctioned traditions. These feelings of guilt may be conscious and spoken about – but such feelings are often unconscious and acted out. And then Jews can become rather demanding that all the arrangements and details of observance are done 'properly', so to speak – as a kind of ritualized compensation for a lapsed connection to the tradition. At least this part of Judaism they can 'get right', even if for the rest of their lives they are living with a nagging awareness that they aren't following their religion the way it's 'supposed' to be done – which is often the way they remember their parents or grandparents doing it. Following a death, adherence to tradition can suddenly become a felt necessity, whatever lack of connection to tradition or community precedes it.

All of which is to say: never underestimate the quirkiness of Jews. The Bible describes the Israelites wandering through the desert as a 'stiff-necked people'. In my experience, I don't think we have changed that much.

So what, in practice, happens when a Jew dies? If there is a deathbed – in a hospital, hospice or at home (that is, unless a death is sudden) – traditional prayers may be recited prior to death, including the recitation of the central prayer of Judaism, the *shema*, a declaration of the Jewish belief in the unity and omnipresence of God: 'Hear, O Israel, the Eternal is our God, the Eternal is One' (Deuteronomy 6.4). Pious Jews through the ages hoped to die with this affirmation on their lips, and although these traditional prayers (sometimes including a formal 'confession of sins') are by no means standard practice nowadays among the majority of Jews, they can bring comfort to the dying and to relatives who may be present. It is a moment when the individual is swallowed up into the larger collective of a faith community and the continuity of its history.

There are no sacramental last rites that need to be administered: the religio-spiritual task is more about creating the best emotionally supportive atmosphere, even if the person is unconscious. It was traditionally seen as a religious duty to stay with the dying so that they do not die alone. And at the point of death the words 'Blessed is the truthful Judge' may be recited by the bystanders, or later when one hears the news of a death one has not witnessed oneself.

Once a death has occurred, Jewish undertakers will be informed by the family in order to arrange a burial in a Jewish cemetery, or a cremation. There are Jewish burial societies who do this work, and voluntary groups called *chevrai kadisha* ('holy brotherhoods/societies') who are sometimes involved in preparing the body for a funeral. Whoever undertakes this, the procedures will be the same: the body is washed and wrapped in a white linen shroud; and it is an ancient tradition that the body should not be left unattended.

It is normative Jewish practice to arrange for the funeral to take place as soon as possible after a death. There are clear historical reasons for this: in the heat of a Middle Eastern climate, body decomposition was obviously an issue, and burials were often arranged on the same day as deaths. And so it became the standard Jewish practice to arrange the funeral within a short period of the death. Nowadays this may be the next day or within a couple of days (sometimes family members need time to travel from across the world), but not on the Sabbath or on Jewish holidays. However distant a Jewish family may be from the traditions of Judaism, there is still a strong cultural pressure at work that says respect for the dead includes making effective arrangements for immediate burial, or as immediate as can be managed.

Jewish funerals and cremations of course take place in ways that intersect with the UK legal requirements of all funerals: the death certificate needs to be taken to the Registrar for Deaths, and the registrar's certificate will then be given to the Jewish burial society, who can't proceed without it. If there is the need for a post-mortem this can delay matters, but the authorities are usually aware of Jewish requirements in relation to burial and will attempt to facilitate as speedily as possible the medical and legal aspects of a post-mortem so as not to cause additional distress for mourners.

A word about cremations: in the Orthodox Jewish community these are not permitted (they were only legalized in Britain in 1884) but they are generally accepted within the Reform and Liberal communities. The reasons why Jewish tradition was opposed to the burning of bodies need not detain us now, but it is an issue that can still generate quite strong feelings among members of the remaining family – an example of how, at the time of a death, a wish to adhere to ancient traditions can come to the fore, even among those who are otherwise secular at heart.

Meanwhile in the mourners' homes there are certain rituals and practices that come into play, a well-worn set of traditions designed psychologically to help people feel they are doing something – when in fact they may be feeling quite helpless and disoriented. A memorial (*yahrzeit*) candle is lit; and in some homes, although it is a practice based on superstition, people will cover all their mirrors. Mourners will customarily remain at home while arrangements for the funeral are being made. Men will stop shaving; traditionally a mourner (male or female) does not wear leather; and in very traditional circles one does not wash either. These are all symbolic signs that one has entered into a period of loss. They are outer markers of separation from daily life and provide a kind of containing framework for the psyche to begin to process the feelings of loss. Most of this processing will of course happen unconsciously, but the outer actions and behaviours provide some structure for the mourning process.

At the funeral itself, mourners gather in the presence of the deceased, who may have been wrapped in her own prayer shawl (*tallit*) prior to being placed in a simple wooden coffin. Elaborate coffins are not permitted – all are equal in death. In traditional communities a symbolic cutting (*k'riah*) is performed on a garment worn by each of the main mourners, a biblically sanctioned action that allows lacerating feelings of grief (or rage) to find a safe outlet in the presence of death. This cutting of an everyday garment like a tie, shirt, jacket or blouse is the outer sign and expression of a universal feeling, echoed in contemporary parlance when someone bereaved may talk of feeling 'all cut up' or 'torn apart' by a death.

When I talk about 'mourners', by the way, although it is obvious that many people may be affected by a death and will be mourning the loss and feeling grief, from a Jewish religious perspective the 'mourners' are certain designated categories: parents, spouses, children and siblings of the deceased. These are the relatives upon whom the traditional ritual acts of mourning devolve.

The funeral service itself is usually short, dignified and marked by an address (*hesped*) that speaks of the life and qualities of the deceased. It is traditional for the person delivering the address to stress the good qualities, merits and achievements of the deceased. But euphemisms are occasionally voiced: 'he was independent minded' usually means he was an awkward old bugger; 'she was feisty' means she had a terrible temper, and so on.

At the heart of the liturgical material recited at a funeral is a traditional prayer called the *Kaddish* ('sanctification'), which is said once a person has died. It speaks of the power of God and the wish for peace and a good life; even the most assimilated and non-observant families know of this prayer and want it said even if, as happens nowadays, they may lack the necessary Hebrew knowledge to be able to read it themselves. The *Kaddish* – which never mentions death but is indelibly associated with it – is deeply ingrained in Jewish consciousness, and the wish to say or hear the words of this ancient prayer is quite independent of religious belief. 'Saying *Kaddish*' is a cultural practice and ritual that is a time-honoured way of plugging into the tradition at this emotionally charged time. Even for the most secular Jew the *wish to believe* may still be lurking in the recesses of the heart. And the *Kaddish* prayer can be the focus for that residual belief, or wish to believe. It may sometimes be the last atavistic remnant of Jewish identity that cannot be surrendered, a lingering emotional connection to the ancestral faith. 'Saying *Kaddish*' reminds us that we are indebted to previous generations whose faith ensured their survival and led them to say *Kaddish* in their turn – and that we are, perhaps in spite of ourselves, one further link in that chain of tradition.

Flowers, incidentally, are not a part of Jewish funerals: they are seen as a kind of artificial cheerfulness. Sometimes I have attended funerals where non-Jewish people have brought flowers and I've seen that they can feel a bit embarrassed when they realize it's not customary to do this. Jewish tradition does encourage the giving of money to charity following a death – this is of more practical benefit than buying flowers, as well as enabling mourners to overcome feelings of helplessness at a time of loss by offering them the experience of doing something that makes a difference.

At the graveside the coffin finds its final resting place in the ground, and both the formal mourners and those gathered around are encouraged to fill in the grave with earth. The hands-on physicality of this can have a powerful impact, as the sight and sound of the earth hitting the coffin makes the finality of the event of death psychologically real. Once the mourners return to the prayer hall and the liturgy concludes, the formal mourners are seated together and the traditional words of hope are spoken that they will be 'comforted with all the mourners of Zion and Jerusalem'. Again, this places an individual loss within the broader context of community and history.

It is traditional too to then greet the mourners individually, and the phrase 'I wish you long life' has become the default greeting among Anglo-Jewry. This is an emotionally complex sentiment that mourners, although they certainly now expect to hear it, may also find difficult to hear in the midst of their grief: it can feel as if the wish is for their upset to be prolonged – although that is exactly the opposite of what the phrase is meant to evoke. In recent years people are finding they want to offer more personalized words of comfort and support at this fraught time – but I don't expect that the standard ritualized greeting will disappear any time soon. It can help to have a set formula to say when one is lost for words.

Time to mourn

Let us magnify and let us sanctify the great name of God in
the world which He created according to His will.
(from the *Kaddish*)

Following the funeral the mourning period proceeds in a familiar pattern. Upon the return from the cemetery a symbolic meal is eaten, including a hard-boiled egg, symbol of the continuity of life. This begins the period of time commonly known by

Jews as 'sitting *shivah*': an initial week-long period of mourning, marked by daily services in the mourner's home, when the mourner traditionally does not go to work but remains indoors and receives visitors who come to pay their respects. It's a time for friends and community to offer comfort and support (and food) and to share their memories of the deceased. For the mourners there is a tradition of sitting on specially designed chairs, low and near the ground. The *yahrzeit* candle, symbolizing the soul of the deceased, remains alight for the whole of this set-apart time. And the *Kaddish* prayer, recited daily, is the religious heart of the mourning period.

Even Jews who might feel rather alienated from other religious practices and traditions will often find themselves embracing these customs (or some of them) following a death. There is a kind of regression happening, a move back to a more basic form of almost tribal practice – small rites and rituals hallowed by memory and tradition that people attach themselves to when faced with the destabilizing emotional turmoil of a death. During these days, as I described earlier in this chapter, all the things said and unsaid start coming to mind, all the regrets and the guilt and the love, the shared experiences and things that could never be shared, all the turbulent chaos of relationships – How close were we? How distant? – all these disparate thoughts and emotions get stirred up in the mourner. Though sometimes there is just a general numbness, unsettling in its own way.

Yet whatever is evoked by a death is held within the ritualized framework of the tradition, and for that week-long period there is nothing else to focus on. And that can be so hard for some people that nowadays some less traditional families have the practice of cutting this period short. They might 'sit *shivah*' for only three nights, or even just one. Busy lives, complex feelings and a traditional world of practice they would rather not engage with, or may no longer feel is a relevant structure for their own process of bereavement. I think this truncating of the tradition is a shame, a lost opportunity, but I acknowledge that we are living in a culture where people have voluntary connections to their religious heritage and feel free (or free-ish) to choose how much or how little they will observe.

So the *shivah* period may be supportive – or it may just feel like it has to be survived so that one can get back to so-called 'normal'. But for those who want to make use of it, the Jewish tradition offers a kind of staged re-entry into the workaday world. One moves in stages from a period of separation to a renewed engagement with the rhythms of ordinary life. The initial seven-day period moves into a second-stage 30-day period (*sh'loshim*) after the funeral, during which people may go back to work but are encouraged not to take part in celebrations, parties and so on. Traditionally one didn't listen to music or buy new clothes in this period; and men continue not to shave as an external sign of their status as mourners.

And then the next stage, beyond the month, is the entire first year after the death, in which one is formally seen by the community as a 'mourner'. During this year one will continue to recite the *Kaddish* memorial prayer when one attends synagogue – and it was traditionally seen as incumbent upon the mourner to attend synagogue with even more rigour than usual, precisely in order to honour the dead through one's personal observance of this requirement to 'say *Kaddish*'. You are remembering the one who has died, and your community is remembering with you. The death is being held in consciousness and the feelings are being processed – there is formal permission, as it were, for them to be processed – as the year unfolds.

Finally, there are two traditional markers of the end of mourning – though of course we know that feelings of loss are independent of these traditional structures designed to contain them. One marker is the so-called 'stone-setting' that in the UK is usually arranged around 11 months after the death, when the mourners revisit the cemetery with family and friends. A tombstone will have been commissioned by the mourners in order to mark the grave formally, and a short service accompanies the unveiling of the stone. During this ceremony the deceased is again recalled in an address, and the inscription, along with the name on the stone, is read aloud.

And then one year on from the death there is the *yahrzeit*, the actual anniversary of the death, when one lights a memorial candle at home – thereby mirroring the opening ritual that immediately followed the death – and the mourner says *Kaddish* for the last time in that year. The time structure I've outlined is like a series of concentric circles emanating out from the original event, and the stages of the process are designed to help with a process of gradual reintegration into life.

But these ripples, a bit like those in a pond, never really cease: *yahrzeit* comes every year on the anniversary of the death, and the *Kaddish* prayer is recited each time. Furthermore, there are memorial services embedded within the Jewish liturgical year – four times a year, including on the Day of Atonement (*Yom Kippur*) – where all those who have ever lost someone recite *Kaddish* in remembrance of those who are no longer with us. (I will say a little more about collective Jewish mourning in the final section of this chapter.) On these occasions an individual's own loss is being held within, and in a sense merged into, the collective acknowledgement that loss is universal, an experience shared by all. There is comfort in knowing we are not alone.

In a larger culture that speaks so glibly of 'closure' and promotes it as a false ideal, Jewish tradition recognizes that losses are real, and lasting: they will happen to you and me, they happen to all of us, and the work of mourning lasts a lifetime. We have to learn to live with our sadness; for as Freud wrote once in a letter:

> we will never find a substitute [after a loss]. No matter what may fill the gap, even if it be filled completely, it nevertheless remains something else. And actually, this is how it should be, it is the only way of perpetuating that love which we do not want to relinquish.

Collective mourning

I form light and create darkness, make peace and create evil:
I, the Eternal, do all these things.

(Isaiah 45.7)

Part of the experience of belonging to a millennia-old faith community is that it can sharpen one's awareness of history. As a Jew I am an inheritor of a multi-generational narrative forged over the centuries in many lands and in many circumstances unimaginably different from my own. This story of the Jewish people is part of my heritage and as such becomes part of how I experience myself in the world. I carry the blessings and the burdens of a particular historical consciousness formed by my understanding of what Jews have done and thought and dreamed, written, recorded and lived, over the centuries – and also what has been done to them over those centuries.

I don't subscribe to the lachrymose view of Jewish history – that the past is merely one long story of suffering and oppression. On the contrary, I see the long-established and persistent Judaic fidelity to tradition, the repeated attempts to live out a particular vision of what God wants of and for humanity, the stubborn refusal to relinquish the hope given to Abraham that we can be a blessing and inspiration to others – I see the whole story and consequences of that fraught and contentious promise as a wondrously vibrant thread in the tapestry of world history. Wrestling with the innate tension between particularism and universalism, Judaism continually promotes the life-affirming potential within humanity; it celebrates the joys – and enunciates the responsibilities – of being alive, of being human, of being created, as the traditional image has it, 'in the image and likeness of God'. So we celebrate the preciousness of life – and, equally, we mourn that life when it is over. And part of the mourning that we do as a community is a mourning not only over individual losses but over the Jewish people's losses. We lament the losses, and we do so collectively.

114

Two days in particular have been set aside in the annual liturgical calendar when we focus on loss and mourn what has occurred, what the Jewish people have endured and Jewish history has witnessed over the millennia. One day is ancient in its provenance; the other is contemporary.

Tisha B'Av – literally 'the ninth day of the Hebrew month *Av*' – is a fast day traditionally seen as the most sorrow-filled of the Jewish calendar. It concludes a three-week period of mourning where the focus is on the destruction of the First and Second Temples in 586 BCE and 70 CE respectively, both of which were finally destroyed, legend has it, on the ninth day of the month of *Av*. Jews have long memories. And even though the final destruction of the cultic centre in Jerusalem by the Romans catalysed a revolutionary era of diasporic Jewish religious creativity – as authority passed from a hierarchical priesthood to an egalitarian rabbinic leadership – the losses associated with the biblically sanctioned institution of the Temple are still remembered with sadness by traditional Jews.

Over time, other tragic events of Jewish significance happened to occur on that date – or came to be associated with that date: the First Crusade was declared on 9th *Av* by Pope Urban II, leading to the decimation of Rhineland Jewry (1095); and on that same date the Jews were expelled from England in 1290, and from the Iberian peninsula in 1492. And so the fast day originally associated with an ancient loss, and with historic Jewish dispersal, accrued to itself over the generations layer after layer of reasons for mourning.

So on *Tisha B'Av* the book of Lamentations is chanted in darkened synagogues to a plaintive melody and special memorial poems of loss are read. Yet the focus is not on individual suffering but on what it means to be part of a people, a collective, who have found themselves suffering for their faith over recorded time. It is as if Jews have eyes thousands of years old, and on this day we face the sombre recognition that, historically, Jewish faith has cost us dear. This we lament, over and again. And yet, undeterred by the pain of collective losses, Jewish hopefulness is still present: rabbinic legend has it that (*pace* the Christian story) it is on *Tisha B'Av* that the Messiah will be born. Judaic myth comes to the rescue in our sorrow, lest it be too much to bear.

And the second day now established in our annual calendar bears witness, paradoxically, to contemporary Jewish religious creativity: *Yom HaShoah*, Holocaust Memorial Day, was inaugurated in Israel in 1953 after the multiple losses suffered by European Jewry during the nightmare years of Nazism. Needless to say, the process of mourning the loss of six million Jews has been a highly complex emotional drama over the last 60 years or so, and the reverberations of those losses continue to disturb the Jewish psyche in ways too convoluted to go into here. It is too soon to tell, but it may be that this partially successful attempt at genocide presents a challenge to the psyche so demanding as to resist an adequate response: are there experiences that are unmournable? Are some losses such an assault upon hopefulness about the human condition that all that is left is lament and more lament? What would it mean to 'recover' from genocide?

But in the context of this chapter, I mention *Yom HaShoah* for its double significance: it is a day set aside in the Jewish calendar for collective mourning; and it exemplifies a very specific situation in which Jewish collective mourning has been, and is often still, fused with individual mourning. For those who suffered directly are still with us. As are their children. And their children's children. All of whom are marked by that suffering.

There are no collectively agreed, religiously sanctioned ways of commemorating the losses. Individual communities mark the day in their own way. In many, survivors of the Holocaust who have lost family and friends join with other Jews whose families may not have been affected personally: the traditional *yahrzeit* candle might be lit by each participant, or a symbolic six candles lit communally; an anthology of Holocaust-related prose and poetry might be assembled and read; there might be the creation of space for those survivors still with us to share their memories and experiences with the next generations; there may be a space too to include the remembrance of other near-genocides (Bosnia, Rwanda) as we lament and mourn our own losses; specific prayers associated in Jewish tradition with death and mourning may be said or sung; and of course the ubiquitous *Kaddish* prayer will be recited.

A solemn note, perhaps, on which to draw this chapter towards a close, but testimony to some inextinguishable desire, resolve, stubbornness, within the Jewish heart: a determination, honed by history and collective temperament, to take seriously the reality of death and loss and the pain of what can never return, while at the same time refusing to fall into hopelessness or despair because of it. Life goes on, will go on, has to go on, regardless. This is not hope beyond the grave but hope in spite of the grave.

Life beyond death?

Whereof one cannot speak, thereof one must be silent.
(Ludwig Wittgenstein)

An afterword. There is something missing from this chapter – although I alluded to it near the beginning of my remarks. Intellectual honesty requires me, prompts me, to return to it, if only briefly. It is actually the question – in one form or another – that I am asked most frequently in pastoral situations surrounding death and mourning: 'Do we Jews believe in life *after* death? Or is this all there is?'

It is of course understandable that the experience of a death prompts these thoughts. Death's stark finality is hard for us to absorb: how can that person, once so physically and emotionally present, be gone, for ever? Surely something of the person – the soul or spirit – lives on? Somehow? Somewhere? Yet for Jews the uncertainty that prompts these questions is also understandable. Because although there have been a variety of views, expressed by generations of rabbis and Jewish philosophers over the last two millennia, there is no unanimity of opinion about this most vexed of questions. What we know is that we can't know what happens next – or if indeed there is any 'next'. Yet the absence of knowledge leaves an emotional vacuum that the imagination cannot help but fill.

Although few hold to this now, two thousand years ago there was a normative view that the dead would be resurrected bodily in the Messianic age; in parallel to this, a Talmudic belief developed, and gained in popularity, that the disembodied soul survived death and lived on – but how and where and in what state was always a matter for speculation, speculation that was often discouraged by the rabbinic authorities in favour of down-to-earthness, getting on with this life and its responsibilities. But rabbinic discouragement never stopped the popular imagination (nor the Jewish mystical tradition) from engaging with this most universal of questions, and a range of folk beliefs and superstitions (like *dybbuks*, dislocated souls) emerged to fill the spaces where the religious authorities refused to go.

What is clear is what people *want* to believe: that there is a truth in the liturgical words that are present in every Jewish prayer service, including the funeral service, when we say 'Blessed are You, Eternal One, who revives the dead'. This traditional translation of a sentiment unambiguously literal in the original Hebrew – *m'cha'yai ha'maytim* – has been modified in some quarters in more recent times to read '. . . who renews life beyond death'. This keeps things vague and open-ended – and introduces a perhaps rather helpful ambiguity about whose life is being referred to: for while we don't know, can't know, the answer to these questions in relation to the one who has gone, we do know, and can trust, that there is the possibility of *a renewal of life beyond death for us who are left* – left to mourn, left to feel the loss and left to find ourselves anew eventually within the reconfigured contours of our own lives. For many Jews (*pace* Wittgenstein) there is comfort and consolation within those traditional words, however they are interpreted. On balance – though this is a moot point – the sentiments they convey can be more help than hindrance within the process of mourning: the wish to be united at some future time with those who are dear to us can seem to be – and in a way is – a denial of the profound painfulness of loss; and yet we can grasp on to such a belief, however haphazardly held, to help compensate for the felt absence of the person who has gone. Whatever our rational minds might tell us, whatever doubts might assail us, people find themselves soothed by the thought that something beyond our understanding is at work: that 'the soul of our dear one is not cut off', that 'love does not die' and that 'truth is stronger than the grave'.

References

Jewish funeral service (2009), *Forms of Prayer V: Funeral Service*, London: Movement for Reform Judaism.

7

Tell me, 'which way ought I to go from here?' Supporting those who grieve in a diverse society

BEN RHODES

As a young child I vividly remember being perplexed because in the middle of a summer's day my grandparents' living room curtains were closed. So I opened them. My granny explained as she closed the curtains again that a woman over the road had died. Closing the curtains was a mark of respect. Although we were not to go to the funeral it was a sign of solidarity – of expressing the family's condolences to the grieving family of a neighbour. As I peeped through the curtains I could see most of the other houses had their curtains shut too.

This was how people in Lincoln, a small provincial city, acknowledged the death of a neighbour in the early 1970s. But things have changed a great deal in the years since. In Britain today, people dying and those who are close to them, or professionals supporting them before and after death, are faced with a multitude of choices and challenges. In this chapter, I want in the current context of diversity to examine some of the spiritual and cultural care resources available to those who grieve and those close to them, or to the professionals who want to support them.

In *Alice in Wonderland*, after following the white rabbit Alice finds herself in a new world. It is a strange space, where things happen to her that are beyond her control and don't fit into her everyday life experience. When she meets the Cheshire Cat sitting on the bough of a tree, Alice goes on to ask: 'Would you tell me, please, which way I ought to go from here?'

'That depends a good deal on where you want to get to,' interjects the cat.

'I don't much care where –' says Alice.

'Then it doesn't matter which way you go,' the cat continues.

'– so long as I get *somewhere*,' Alice adds as an explanation.

'Oh, you're sure to do that,' says the cat, 'if you only walk long enough.'

Supporting someone about to be bereaved or who is already bereaved can feel very like the interaction of Alice and the cat. As family member, friend or professional you can encounter someone disorientated, whose world has changed – sometimes beyond recognition. Those who grieve may be so affected or shocked by events that they don't know how to make the next step, and stumble from one thing to another. There can seem too many 'oughts', which can add to feelings of sadness, shock, anger, low mood, guilt, stress or burden – these 'rights and wrongs' somehow enter the consciousness of the grieving person. And those alongside the grieving person are uncertain as to the origins of such rights and wrongs, or why the person feels that they need to be heeded. There may be uncertainty about what the family and friends, the healthcare professional, social worker, chaplain, parish priest, bereavement counsellor are supposed to do, or how they might help. The challenge is to identify with great sensitivity what is helpful and beneficial to those grieving, and to allow them to negotiate their journey as well as possible in this new terrain.

Changing contexts

Britain has changed greatly over the last 250 years. Danny Boyle's imaginative opening ceremony at the London 2012 Olympics dramatically portrayed some of the social changes that have made the society we see in Britain today: the shift for the majority from rural to urban life, often requiring a move away from extended family support for work; an economy that has helped to create a diverse population with many different ethnicities, beliefs and cultures. Walking down my local high street in south-east London I see a rich and vibrant mix of people: white and black, Afro-Caribbean and African, Indian and Pakistani, Greek, Portuguese and Eastern European. I sample different cuisines, buy exotic fruit and vegetables, encounter many faiths and beliefs. These changes in society have been mirrored in the way of death, dying and grief, and the many ways Britain approaches these today.

In the twentieth and twenty-first centuries the Victorian world of 'oughts' has become one of diverse choice. This diversity of approach can be really helpful in freeing some people to grieve in the way that is supportive to them, while for others the passing of a homogenized approach has diminished the resources they can use to grieve effectively. For those supporting the bereaved, increasing diversity can be a challenge but also an opportunity.

Supporting those who are bereaved

Before going further it is perhaps helpful to establish what I mean by 'spiritual' and 'cultural'. McSherry and Ross (2010) demonstrate in a literature search of nursing papers that at least 92 definitions of spirituality exist. This is no surprise. Go into any bookshop or read any weekend supplement – the word 'spiritual' appears frequently, and clearly has multiple meanings. In 2011 the Royal College of Nursing produced an excellent guide to spiritual care. Its usefulness goes way beyond the nursing profession and healthcare, as it clearly and concisely describes what spirituality is about. I use here Speck's definition of spiritual as 'A search for existential meaning within a life experience, with reference to a power other than the self, which may not be called "God"' (Speck, 1998). In essence, spiritual matters are those that give shape and meaning to people's lives, whether or not such matters stand in relation to a transcendent reality.

Making sense of the world and our place in it is something we do all the time. What does it mean to be a human being? What does it mean to love and be loved? What happens at death? What's it all about? Clearly these questions come into sharper focus when someone significant in our lives dies, and when through grieving we are adjusting to what life is about after that person's death. Religion takes these ultimate questions and struggles with them through holy text, ritual and rites of passage. Defining spirituality in this way means all religious care should be spiritual, but not all spiritual care is necessarily religious. It also makes explicit that all people, religious and non-religious, potentially have spiritual needs. If someone understands themselves as atheist, humanist or agnostic, professionals should be aware of the potential need to support that person just as much as someone with a practising faith.

The *Concise Oxford Dictionary* defines culture as 'the ideas, customs, and social behaviour of a particular people or society'. Closely linked, but important to differentiate, is ethnicity. The website <www.ethnicityonline.net> defines an ethnic group as 'a community of people who share cultural and/or physical characteristics including one or more of the following: history, political system, religion, language, geographical origin, traditions, myths, behaviours, foods, genetic similarities and physical features'. Sikhs and Jews are clear examples of peoples whose culture is also very important to their identity.

In July 2012 the Department of Health published its first ever survey of bereaved relatives in England. The survey asked them about the care received in the last three months of their relative's life and across a number of settings: home, hospice and hospital, and in the community. The report paints a positive picture of the quality of end-of-life care but significantly shows that satisfaction with emotional and spiritual support received in the last two days of life ranked lower than other measures, with 15 per cent of bereaved relatives and 19 per cent of carers rating the care of the dying patient and their own care as 'poor'. This snapshot demonstrates the need for professionals to consider the spiritual and cultural needs of people who are dying, and of those who support them, and to address these more carefully.

The greatest asset for anyone seeking to support the bereaved is their own humanity. For someone grieving, no words can adequately express all that is happening. In fact there is a danger that we try to fill what we perceive as an uncomfortable silence with words – which is more about our own needs than those of the bereaved. Frequently what is required is simply to sit alongside someone. The implicit question the bereaved person may be asking is, 'Can you hold my pain and distress?' Grief can be very isolating, even if those who mourn have many people around them. On occasions bereaved people notice that some avoid them for fear of upsetting them. Whatever someone's culture or belief, it is important to acknowledge what has happened, and to listen to what people are saying, in a way that is appropriate to the personal or professional relationship with that grieving person.

Society seems to talk less these days about death, dying and bereavement, even though it is the one event that we can guarantee will happen to us all. This lack of openness can burden the bereaved and stifle support. An organization called Dying Matters is trying to change this: <www.dyingmatters.org> has some really useful advice for individuals and professionals who are trying to meet spiritual and cultural needs. It emphasizes the importance of attentive presence, of asking what someone needs, of listening and responding. This is surely vital to any effective support. Sometimes it will not be possible to meet all needs, and the process is sometimes about finding strategies together that may be of help, even if only partially.

Death comes in many ways, expected and unexpected, suddenly or after a long illness. When death can be anticipated, the grieving process for some can be helped through preparation, both before death and afterwards. In South London the health service is rolling out a system called the AMBER care bundle (see <ambercarebundle.org>), which was developed at Guy's and St Thomas' NHS Foundation Trust. This system works by identifying patients who are likely to die within the next few months and then – as far as individuals and their carers wish to – talking about their wishes and what is important to them. This may include spiritual and cultural matters.

Within the hospice movement are many excellent multi-professional teams, determining and striving where possible to meet individuals' holistic needs. Advance care plans – which may include limits on treatment, along with the individual's preferred place of death and spiritual, social and cultural needs – are increasingly being used in the hospice sector; and there are lessons to be learned elsewhere. Having these conversations earlier can mean a better death for people, and may later be a comfort and help to the bereaved.

When a person's death is imminent the Liverpool Care Pathway (see <liv.ac.uk/mcpcil/liverpool-care-pathway>) is another resource becoming more widely used in hospitals. It is not, as some faith groups and sections of the press have suggested, a way of bringing euthanasia into the health system. Developed in Liverpool, it is on the contrary a tool that brings a dying person's needs together holistically. It covers cultural and spiritual needs about which it is mandatory to ask the patient or, if that is not possible, those close to the patient. The Pathway covers the periods before, at and after death, and is designed to allow professionals to identify and try to facilitate what is important to the people involved. One change that does seem to be making a difference is the efforts of health and social care professionals to carry out a dying person's wishes regarding the place of his or her death. At present most deaths in Britain occur in hospital. It is recognized that this is not what most people – and those close to them – desire. The term used is 'preferred priorities in care'. It is becoming routine for multi-professional teams to try to discharge people rapidly from hospital or hospice and to allow them to die at home, or some other place of their choosing, if that is what the person wishes.

It is essential to consider the language used around and after death, as it can have a significant impact on how people grieve. In situations where bad news has to be broken, such as sudden death in an emergency department, it is vital to communicate the reality of a death sensitively but clearly. Euphemisms such as 'I'm sorry we have lost your mum' don't help the bereaved and can lead to misunderstanding. For example, if the mother had dementia and her son or daughter had no knowledge of what had happened, on hearing this form of words they might reasonably think their mother had evaded staff and walked out of the department, to be lost on the street. Other comments, such as 'He's gone to a better place' or 'Jesus wanted her for an angel', may bring comfort to some, but if you don't believe in any afterlife – or indeed even if you do – they might be highly offensive. Equally, many newly bereaved relatives will turn to me as a Christian chaplain and on their own initiative want some sense to be made of what has happened to their relative. This too needs listening and dialogue and, where appropriate, talking about Christian hope.

Conversely, for us as professionals, sensitivity is required if a relative uses some of the phrases above. It may be that the bereaved are not in denial and that a particular understanding gives them hope and comfort. It is only later, if people get 'stuck' in grief, that support may be needed. For example, it is the practice of some African Christians or Muslims to use certain forms of words, even before death. It is every Muslim's duty to wish another Muslim a long and healthy life. To a professional who hears those close to a patient saying these words when she has just spent hours explaining their brother is dying, this may seem frustrating – and the assumption may be that the relatives are in denial. Perhaps they are, but equally they may have taken on board all that has been discussed and are just following convention. Equally, after a similar discussion a Nigerian family may start talking about the power of miracles and call the chaplain to give hope and encourage a grandmother. Again, it may be denial – but, more likely, in some African cultures you would not tell someone they are going to die. As a chaplain I have seen too many professionals insisting that an open conversation be had with the dying patient and family, and either feeling stonewalled or meeting great anger and upset that adds later to the family's grief. Things need to be checked carefully: would it be better to have the conversation with the family away from the bedside? Is the patient actually saying she doesn't want to know her diagnosis? For a better outcome, conversations need to be held in a way that considers the culture and spirituality of those concerned.

For some cultures and faiths, throughout life and perhaps especially at death, being cared for by a person of the same gender is important. This may be for reasons of dignity or ritual cleanliness. At times this isn't possible, and in such cases a chaperone can help. On a simple level this could involve hand-shaking, which some Jews (usually Orthodox and ultra-Orthodox) and Muslims do not do with the opposite sex. Sometimes it is being in a room with a person of the opposite sex without a family member being present, which can make things even more difficult if a sensitive or confidential matter is to be discussed. Some people, however, may be happy to shake hands or have a conversation with someone of the opposite gender. In all aspects of spiritual and cultural care it is important that we don't label people or see care as an 'us and them' situation. We need to celebrate their differences and allow space for them to be who they are, rather than see them as stereotypes.

Resourcing professionals

Dame Cicely Saunders, a doctor and the founder of the modern hospice movement, said, 'How people die remains in the memory of those who live on.' The support and care that is given to people around death has a direct impact on those who grieve. It is vital that those who support them strive to ensure good holistic care, to which people's culture and spirituality are fundamental. But where can we look for help at those times when we are unsure?

The foundation of good support lies deep within us. It is not necessary to commit to memory every detail of human spirituality and belief. It starts with establishing good rapport and being empathetic. In the face of death and grief, or perhaps of our own discomfort – or even just under the pressure of wanting to do our very best – there is a danger of resorting to books, lists or websites. The best care is achieved by establishing what another person needs, and then actively listening and working on that person's behalf to meet those needs as far as possible. Books, web links and policies can be good at establishing what a faith believes and teaches about death and dying, and its practices after death. When it comes to supporting people, it is important to remember that even though they may appear orthodox in their belief and practice, many in fact choose to live their faith out in very different ways from what is prescribed, and may feel judged or not heard if they are treated as if they are textbook examples of, say, a Muslim or humanist. The two Orthodox Jewish men in the room may not be brothers but civil partners, who are not only facing the reality that death will soon separate them but wondering how others in the community will react after one of the partners has died.

It is vital when supporting the dying and bereaved never to assume, but to ask. This may seem clichéd, but in high-stress situations it is very easy to slip into assumptions inadvertently. However, resources are excellent help in preparing to talk to someone. Additionally it can be an asset to have some basic understanding of psychology and the work of Elisabeth Kübler-Ross and Colin Murray Parkes. The same is true here, in that we need to see grief as a normal part of the human condition and not to pathologize individuals; but it can help to think about more intensive support if the grieving process is complex or gets stuck, as we are concerned with caring for the whole person rather than compartmentalizing bits of him.

Organizational policies can help throughout end-of-life care, especially when a dying person cannot communicate his or her wishes and there is no one to ask. Hospital end-of-life policies often have appendices on spiritual and cultural support. These can be used when spiritual and cultural needs have been established. For many faiths, what happens to a person before and after death may have implications for that person in whatever is believed to follow. For Roman Catholics and some in the Church of England, the chance of not having 'the sacrament of the sick' before death can cause much distress, as the dying person may well be perceived as having been denied the chance to be reconciled and commended to God.

Care of those who have died, which is sometimes called laying out or last offices, should reflect cultural and spiritual needs. For Jews and Muslims, and among some other people of faith, it is important that the body is not washed. The gender of those performing the last offices is also important for dignity, and sometimes for reasons of ritual purity. Done well, care of a person can reassure those who have been bereaved. If done incorrectly, however, in addition to potentially causing religious offence it can add to grief and may have a longer-term impact.

There are many good books covering cultural and spiritual care. One of the best resources is on the internet, produced by NHS Scotland Education: *Spiritual Care: A Multi-Faith Resource for Healthcare Staff*. It is a well-written piece that covers the main points likely to be needed in supporting others, and one that I personally have found helpful.

Another source of support for professionals is to be found with local faith leaders. It is important to have checked with those you are supporting what they need, and also if they are happy to be referred to other people for help. Usually each borough or county has an inter-faith forum (sometimes called a multi-faith forum). A good example would be the website <www.faithstogetherinlambeth.org>, through which a number of faith groups can be contacted.

If local contacts do not work, <www.mfghc.com> (the multi-faith group for healthcare chaplaincy) has a variety of resources and links to the world faiths. In my experience this is a good way to contact someone from a less familiar belief organization or tradition within a world faith. The Buddhist Society, for example, is able to suggest local contacts within Buddhism's different traditions. Healthcare or higher-education chaplains are also worth contacting, as they often have good links with competent representatives from faith organizations.

What about those who don't follow a world faith? Having defined spirituality in terms of shape and meaning, I would argue that all people potentially have needs to be assessed and met. Bereavement is about facing the new realities of life. Often I think there is an assumption that the non-religious have no spiritual needs, and that chaplains and religious leaders will therefore have no interest in caring for and supporting them. In thinking about supporting the bereaved within the public services, other professionals can help allay fears. As a hospital chaplain I am not allowed to proselytize – even if I might wish to. Within the community, hospice chaplains and other pro-fessionals can usually, with consent, make referrals to people who can support the bereaved. Sometimes humanist or non-religious people are happy to see chaplains and know they will be respected; for others, seeing a non-religious person is essential. The British Humanist Association (BHA) has been happy to send an experienced person to talk with someone from a non-religious perspective.

Having signposted resources, I want to present some scenarios that raise issues around dying, death and grief.

Supporting bereaved Christian Afro-Caribbean families through funeral rites

Traditionally, although there will be differences in the liturgy in each denomination, any minister or priest may expect to be asked to support an Afro-Caribbean person in the following ways. Prayers will be offered for nine nights before the funeral service, and the minister will definitely be expected to attend on at least one of those nights – either the first or the last – or maybe even on all nine. On the morning of the funeral the priest or minister will go to the family home to pray with the chief mourners. Whatever their denomination, the members of the family and friends of the person who has died will give eulogies. The coffin will also be open for viewing, allowing all present to pay their final respects. The person is usually buried, and after the committal all present stay to sing hymns while the grave is backfilled and the flowers laid on top. The funeral party then goes for a meal, which cannot start until the minister says the table blessing. The minister will be expected to stay throughout the reception, to be available to anyone who wishes to talk.

Considering the traditions of Afro-Caribbean families also illustrates the changes that have taken place in Britain over the last decades, and the need to identify what people actually need. Traditions change, so the expectations described above may not hold true. Church colleagues based in the community are reporting anecdotally that third-generation black British people are choosing not to have all the ceremonies their grandparents and parents did. Instead many people are opting to have a service at the cemetery or crematorium.

Baby deaths and funerals

I remember reading about an archdeacon and his wife in a Susan Howatch 'Starbridge' novel. Howatch vividly paints the events leading up to a stillbirth and the impact on the mother

131

and her husband. The archdeacon's wife wasn't allowed to see – let alone hold – her child, carried in her womb for all those months. This was done supposedly for her benefit, to avoid distress. The archdeacon, I guess unusually for the time, held prayers for the child. The impact of what was then standard practice, but would now be very differently handled, cast a deep shadow over their lives: deep, acute grief that was hard to resolve.

Today things are very different for women who miscarry, have a stillborn child or have a termination of pregnancy. There may be specialist midwives to support, and especially facilitate, culturally and spiritually appropriate care. The woman and those with her will have a choice whether to see the baby or not. The baby may be washed and dressed. Handprints and footprints could be taken – maybe a lock of hair. Photographs too are possible, but some cultures and some faiths find it inappropriate. In one hospital where I worked, many Bengali women, through cultural convention, preferred not to have pictures, while others found them a comfort. The challenge for professionals is to give the mother the choice, asking in a way that is not offensive, but is right for her.

As healthcare chaplains we are often called to 'bless' dead babies, either with or without the parents present. This may be a religious rite, including prayers for the baby, the grieving mother and the wider support network. It may also include the naming of the child, although some mothers prefer not to name babies (for example, mothers of African heritage, as this is something that happens days after the birth and has its own cultural and religious pattern). Or it may be a non-religious ceremony to acknowledge the death, and at which the parents might talk of their hopes and feelings. As chaplains we will give 'blessing' cards to affirm the reality of the child and offer something to remember it by, in a place where there perhaps seems little to hold on to.

The death of a baby is not uncommon; sadly, in Britain a quarter of pregnancies do not end with a live birth. Yet it can bring a woman and any partner an increased sense of isolation and lack of support. In a society that finds grief difficult, this can seem impossible to bear. There are some excellent support organizations, including SANDS, the Stillbirth and Neonatal Death Society. SANDS has done a huge amount in recent years to support the bereaved and also to press for change. Some parents will choose to arrange the funeral for their baby; others will opt for the hospital to make the arrangements. Again here, hospital chaplains will try to support parents in their wishes. One thing I had to learn quickly was that the parents may not necessarily turn up. People of all backgrounds have the choice, and some feel they don't wish to, or can't, attend. I have noticed that many African families do not attend – or that only the husbands attend; and often Muslim parents do not attend. A colleague of African heritage explained that, culturally, women are not permitted to attend, and a Muslim colleague explained that the soul is understood in Islam to enter the baby at a certain point in pregnancy; before this point some parents would not consider it necessary to attend a funeral.

Memorial services

Many hospices and hospitals have memorial services or events to celebrate a life; they can be for babies, children and adults. They seem to be growing in popularity and, as fewer people practise a faith, the numbers seem to be going up. It is important to remember too the excellent memorial services held by faith groups, inviting those to whom they have given support through funerals.

In all the services I have been associated with, a multi-professional approach is taken in planning and attendance. For the bereaved, seeing people who have cared for a significant person who has died and being able to tell them how they are getting on now seems to be appreciated. It also allows people to ask for help if they need it – often the tea and coffee afterwards is important for this – or to meet others who have faced bereavement. For parents whose baby or child has died it is vital, and many report that this is the only place where they feel they can be themselves – that they are understood.

Each ceremony has a mixture of religious and non-religious readings. Elizabeth Jennings' poem beginning 'What ceremony can we fit/You into now?' is excellent for babies' and children's ceremonies. A choice of music is also important. It always seems best to represent a diversity of culture and spirituality that allows a number of access points. This is much more meaningful than trying for the lowest common denominator, which means nothing to anyone and gives no tools for grieving. There seems to be a range of symbols that are appreciated: the lighting of candles; perhaps creating something using flowers, seeds or stones. A word of caution here: for some Muslims, candles are not helpful. For some Jewish people, stones are commonly used, but flowers are not regarded as appropriate. Sometimes books of remembrance can be used in the ceremony; names can be read; photographs or items important to the person who has died can be brought. In one health trust where I worked we used the cathedral, but as there was a large Muslim population it was important to hear a Middle Eastern instrument, such as an oud, being played, to make people feel welcome. Since the death of Diana, Princess of Wales, when thousands and thousands of floral tributes were laid outside London palaces, finding a place where death can be marked seems to have become more important in people's journey of grief. Since 1997 it has become increasingly common to see flowers by the roadside, often fastened to railings or posts, and signifying the location of an accident.

Organ donation

Organ donation can focus the spiritual and cultural needs of the dying and bereaved. In Britain, NHS Blood and Transplant (NHSBT) is the organization that oversees the voluntary system of donation of organs, tissue, stem cells and blood. It has a number of nurses specializing in organ donation, embedded in hospitals that work with wider professional teams for the benefit of donors and recipients. The nurses are trained to approach those close to potential organ donors, and facilitate a conversation that helps them arrive at a definite no or yes – a decision they can live with for the rest of their lives.

Six of the world faiths represented in Britain have produced guides with NHSBT that in general support organ donation and that are available through the organ donation website. (Jehovah's Witnesses and Taoism are two of the few faiths that prohibit organ donation.) The Organ Donation Campaign with the Department of Health report is informed directly from focus groups of people belonging to various faith groups. The report highlights the many challenges faced in the UK. If you are Afro-Caribbean, black African or have heritage from the Indian subcontinent, the chances are that you will have to wait considerably longer for an organ to be donated to save your life. Essentially, a need to educate faith leaders was identified, so that they in turn could support people making decisions as to whether or not to allow a relative to become a donor. In Afro-Caribbean and African cultures, as for Muslims and Jews, there can be concerns about keeping the body uncut. In African and Afro-Caribbean cultures there can be questions about whether people will be able to be raised in the afterlife if organs are missing. There is much more work to be done and NHSBT is starting new workstreams, both to work with people's cultural and spiritual needs and to answer their concerns. Having said this, I have known people from all of the above-mentioned groups allow donation. Again, people don't always live out their faith and culture as we might expect.

Being a donor can bring great comfort and help to some families in their grief. Recently, Tom Heffer, who was a priest, died. He and his family were all lifelong supporters of donation. In a newspaper report his widow spoke very movingly about the donation:

Mrs Heffer, 57, said the news brought great comfort to her family, despite their grief. 'When I knew there was nothing more they could do for Tom, I hung on to the fact that there was a family somewhere that was going to get a call in the middle of the night to say: 'We have a kidney for you'. In the whole context of what has happened, that was something I tried to imagine. That was why Tom carried a card. It was what he wanted.

(*Eastern Daily Press*, 2012)

So much has changed in Britain that old patterns of death, dying and grief have been lost and new ones have emerged. This has perhaps been most pronounced when considering spiritual and cultural care. For those seeking to support others, contemporary society is incredibly diverse, requiring many different approaches. The situations and approach I have written about here are not the definitive word on spiritual and cultural care. I get things wrong, but I hope when that is the case that I have the humility to apologize.

For the sake of those we have the privilege to walk alongside and support, it is essential we seek to strive for true holistic care with the dying and bereaved – care that values and attends to their spirituality and culture. The basis of all good spiritual and cultural care is humanity. There are many resources that can help and guide us, but these need to be used alongside sensitive enquiry about needs, attentive listening, empathy in trying to respond to what is asked of us, and honesty in explaining the limits of what is possible. Through reflecting on our own needs and experience of death and grief, we can come to appreciate the needs and choices others have made, no matter how different from our own.

Resources and further reading

The British Humanist Association has published two books: *Thinking about Death* and *Funerals Without God*. See <humanism.org.uk>.
<endoflifecareforadults.nhs.uk>, the National End of Life Programme, is a Department of Health website covering all aspects of end-of-life care including cultural and spiritual care.

<ethnicityonline.net> is a website with useful information to help professionals deliver culturally appropriate care.

Hollins, S. (2009), *Religions, Culture and Healthcare*, Milton Keynes: Radcliffe Publishing.

Jogee, Moussa E., ed. (2004), *Religions and Cultures: A Guide to Beliefs, Customs and Diversity for Health and Social Care Services*, Edinburgh: R&C Publications.

Kübler-Ross, Elisabeth (2005), *On Grief and Grieving: Finding the Meaning of Grief Through the Five Stages of Loss*, London: Simon & Schuster.

Murray Parkes, Colin (2010), *Bereavement: Studies of Grief in Adult Life*, 4th edn, London: Penguin.

NHS Blood and Transplant faith guides can be found at <www.organdonation.nhs.uk/ukt/how_to_become_a_donor/religious_perspectives/religious_perspectives.asp>

NHS Scotland, <www.nes.scot.nhs.uk/media/3723/spiritualcarematters-final.pdf> is an excellent resource for professionals to think about care they are giving; also <www.nes.scot.nhs.uk/media/3720/march-07finalversions.pdf.pdf>, which is one of the most valuable multi-faith resources available.

Royal College of Nursing (2011), *Spirituality in Nursing Care: A Pocket Guide*, downloadable at <www.rcn.org.uk/__data/assets/pdf_file/0008/372995/003887.pdf>

References

Eastern Daily Press (2012), <www.edp24.co.uk/news/health/bishop_of_norwich_s_late_chaplain_gave_gift_of_life_through_organ_donation_1_1451027#>

McSherry, W. and Ross, L., eds (2010), *Spiritual Assessment in Health Care Practice*, Keswick: M&K Publishing.

Speck, P. (1998), 'The Meaning of Spirituality in Illness', in Cobb, M. and Robshaw, V., eds, *The Spiritual Challenge of Healthcare*, Edinburgh: Churchill Livingstone.

8

Inside the grief of soldiers and their families: an army chaplain's experience

RICHARD M. SMITH

The Royal Army Chaplains' Department has commissioned ordained clergy into its ranks since 1796. Its task through the centuries has been to offer spiritual support, moral guidance and pastoral care in the most extreme of circumstances. The chaplain's parish becomes the military unit within which he or she works; the chaplain is sent not to a place, but to a group of people. As each military unit deploys throughout the world, its chaplain accompanies it as its soldiers fulfil their mission. A non-combatant and therefore never armed, he or she stands as a sign of peace in the midst of war.

As one such chaplain, I hope to share with you some key themes from my work within the Army over the past decade. My experiences are not particularly unusual and include work in Iraq, Afghanistan and the UK. I hope that my thoughts on these matters may be useful to others who deal with situations of an extreme nature.

A chaplain's experience

In this first section, I want to consider three aspects of the chaplain's work. First I intend to discuss the shock experienced by those who witness, or are close to, the violent death of colleagues. Second I shall consider the formal and informal rituals around death and grief. Finally I will look specifically at the chaplain's role and the need to try to be in the right place at the right time.

The shock of death

While all death has some element of shock about it, the death of a soldier is often followed by particularly deep shock and disbelief. I recall a number of instances, some on operations and some in the UK, where this has been the case. Young soldiers especially, it seems to me, move very quickly into an almost frozen state of shock. Sometimes they appear to exhibit a trance-like state that only time and space can heal. As the chaplain, it has often been my task to sit with them as they thaw back into normality and are ready to face the world again.

To sit with someone in this situation is both unpredictable and a privilege. Time becomes irrelevant and yet over time words and emotions begin to resurface. In my experience the most common word in these situations is: 'Why?' Why did this happen? Why was it him not me? Why did they do that? Why? Why? Why? To all such questions there are few simple answers.

My ministry to soldiers such as these has been to accept the silence and not to fill it with meaningless nonsense; to allow them to think in dignity and privacy and to have the confidence not to speak. There is in such moments a shared acknowledge-ment of emptiness and helplessness. These soldiers' grief is almost always fuelled by anger, disbelief, guilt and pain. For my part, I have become acutely aware that no words I can say will make sense of these various chaotic events; there is no way of putting things back or making things right. It is always a mess that we who are left behind have to live with.

I often find that I am held between the desire to speak and the need to allow the silence to minister in its own way. This is true of all speech, but especially true when it comes to prayer. While there are many moments when my role as a chaplain is not overtly religious, at other moments it is clearly appropriate to lead the soldiers in a spiritual act. Such an act might not be religiously specific, but universal and inclusive. Discerning the right and wrong moment to speak or pray is the really difficult part. Yet being too scared of failure is not helpful to anyone.

When appropriate, prayer has a power that is hard to define. In those difficult situations of pain and grief, somehow a simple prayer makes available to those present a spiritual well from which they draw solace and comfort. In these moments tears are common. Most of my soldiers are not devoutly religious, but a prayer to God in the midst of shock and grief appears to matter, and matter profoundly.

Each of the situations I have dealt with has been different, but on every occasion there has been a moment when it is appropriate to guide the grieving soldier back into the care of his friends. For some this has been within hours, for others it has been longer, but at some point the protective bubble around the soldier must be broken and he or she must reintegrate. It is at this point that the soldiers frequently surprise me. As you will probably be aware, soldiers can be brash, full of bravado, arrogant and rude, but in moments like these they gather as a family would, care for each other and in their own way work through their collective grief with black humour and heartfelt sincerity.

My experience is that soldiers always seem to recover from their grief, however unlikely that seems in those first moments. They appear to appreciate the military and religious rituals the Army expects and in time, with support, they are able to continue in their chosen career. Deep down I suspect that they never forget, that they are never quite the same people as they would have been otherwise, but then who is?

The formal and informal rituals around grief

As a Methodist minister this is an area I feel less qualified to comment on than most. Yet my experience within the Army suggests that what we do in the form of ritual is as important, if not more important, than the words we use.

During the last decade I have been asked on numerous occasions to pray with those who are dying or who have just died. Such events are always difficult. The words I use are based on a service from the *Methodist Worship Book* (Methodist Church of Great Britain, 1999, pp. 426–32), but in a sense the specific words don't seem to matter. What matters most is that due dignity and respect is paid to a person who is passing or has passed from this world to the next. These last rites take many forms in different churches and in different faiths, and views will vary as to the effect such a service has on the deceased. My experience is that the families of those who have died are always grateful that in those moments when they couldn't be there, a chaplain was able to minister in such a way. While these prayers do not help a family avoid their grief, they seem to bring some comfort that would otherwise not be present.

In the case of a death on operations, the grief of the soldier's friends is intertwined with formal repatriation, the process of sending a deceased soldier back to his family in the UK. This process of military ritual and practical transportation has varied hugely over the years due to situation and circumstance. It is always important to the soldiers and their commanders that all due dignity and military honour be afforded to the deceased. While all soldiers find these things difficult, they seem to use such practical elements to afford worth to the deceased and come to terms with their own emotions.

The formal military funeral is used in a similar way. A military unit will prepare and rehearse at great length in order to 'perform' the rituals in as perfect a manner as possible. While in normal circumstances these things would not be so important, at a military funeral they are seen as a way of honouring the person who has died and a practical, physical way of demonstrating how much that person means to the whole group.

Although such actions are not a 'cure' for deep-rooted grief, they appear to have a therapeutic effect.

In addition to the formal rituals, the modern British Army has adopted some informal ways of honouring its dead and dealing with its members' own emotions. During my time in Iraq and Afghanistan it was usual for memorial services to be held for those who had died. These events were in the framework of a religious service with hymns and readings, but focused also on remembering the person who had died. On numerous occasions a tribute was given that would make most church congregations cringe, but was perfect for the soldiers present. Stories and tales of adventures were told and heartfelt messages sent to a friend no longer present. Once more, these events went some way to verbalizing the inner grief of the soldier community; they didn't solve anything as such, but people felt that they had done what needed to be done and they felt better for it. The commanders with whom I worked also saw the benefit of these services; they seemed to frame a moment and allow the soldiers to let go, to move on enough to continue the mission.

The soldiers also work through their grief with more informal rituals. The most common of these are related to drinking. A frequent practice, one that often takes place when a group of soldiers returns to the UK after losing a colleague in battle, is to buy the deceased a pint of beer and at the end of the evening stand in a circle and pass the beer around, each taking a sip and recalling a moment they spent with their friend. I imagine such simple, informal ritualistic recollections are extremely common and mean a great deal to those involved. Just like Roman, Celtic and Viking warriors, our soldiers drink together in joy and sorrow.

Being in the right place at the right time

One of the keys to effective military chaplaincy is being in the right place at the right time, and at the same time accepting that this is not always possible. Throughout the last decade there have been many moments where I have sensed that I have been in the right place, but many, many more where I have felt frustrated about being unable to be where I might bring some comfort.

As military chaplains we are able to locate and relocate in order to care effectively for our people. On a number of occasions I have found it important to base my ministry alongside those who are vulnerable and grieving. Soldiers do not receive time off to grieve but routinely continue with their duties, and often need support as they do so. The skill is in being available, while not being too visible or obvious. In this way soldiers feel supported and able to carry on, but not mothered or imposed upon in any way. Similarly I have found that the commanders of the Army at all levels are able to rest more assured if their chaplains are readily available to those who might need them most. Once again this adds to the healing process and offers a spiritual and emotional safety net.

In these situations many soldiers come to the chaplain to speak about how they are feeling. Some speak about their regrets, their questions, their fear and their guilt. Others come because they are experiencing grief for the first time and they are not sure whether their emotions and physical sensations are normal. Such conversations are not necessarily religious, but are born out of the Church's desire to care for the soldier's most human needs. Sometimes prayer is appropriate, sometimes not. Some soldiers want to talk about heaven, others suspect there is nothing but darkness. Each soldier, religious or not, uses the chaplain to process his or her thoughts and adjust to a new reality, which sadly often includes the pain of loss and the process of grief.

The need to be in the right place at the right time is fairly obvious, but as a chaplain one has more opportunity to choose one's place than in a traditional ministry setting. Through discernment and experience one can learn to read the signs and be as much help as possible.

A chaplain's reflections

In this second section, I shall reflect upon the privileged position of the Army chaplain in the hope that it might be useful to those in other ministerial fields. As chaplains we are part of the different units we serve, but not completely controlled by the leaders of those units. Each chaplain is sent by his church to work in the Army, and it is from the church that we derive our authority to minister. (All full-time uniformed chaplains are presently Christian, and are hence sent by a church. The Ministry of Defence employs a Civilian Chaplain to the Military for Muslims, Buddhists, Hindus, Sikhs and Jews.) This means that we must balance the tension between two masters, the Church (and through it God) and the Army (a tool of the state). This duality might be seen as a disadvantage, yet in fact it allows the chaplain to sit outside the regular Army chain of command and to be one of the very few who is able to critique others with authority. This means that in organizational terms the chaplain is in the unit, but not of the unit. We are there with very different motivations, often with different backgrounds, and with slightly different aims to be achieved. Why does this matter? It matters because the only way to minister to soldiers is to be inside the boundaries of their organization. It means to wear their uniform, adopt their language, understand their frustrations and sometimes share their dangers. This duality enables a level of pastoral, spiritual and moral care that would not be possible as a civilian. Within the Army a civilian is almost always seen as an outsider.

When one considers soldiers' reaction to grief, our ability to work from within their organization is greatly advantageous. It means that they do not have to explain everything to us, and that they presume a certain amount of knowledge and understanding about the context in which they live and work. One of the key differences between grief in the Army on operations and grief within the civilian population is that soldiers are rarely given enough time at the moment in question to grieve; they are required to put their emotions to one side and continue with their mission. I recall with sadness the frequent deaths of soldiers during my tours of Afghanistan; it nearly always felt that both the unit and the individual soldiers had not recovered from the death of a friend before another friend was killed. This relentless attack on the emotions causes soldiers to become ever more numb to their own feelings. While they can be very resilient in the short term, it seems to me that many are simply delaying their period of grieving until their tour is over, at which point they can surrender themselves to their heightened emotions. Over the years both chaplains and Army welfare staff have had to respond to the aggressive 'fall-out' from combat operations once the soldiers have returned to their home garrisons. This fall-out comprises difficulties in relationships, an increase in violent alcohol-related incidents and a recklessness on the roads that may lead to all too many unnecessary further deaths. Much of this flows from grief and the soldiers' natural reactions to traumatic situations. Thankfully most soldiers return to relative 'normality' within a matter of months.

One of the common ongoing issues once soldiers have returned home is what is known as a 'grief ambush'. This is an inevitable occurrence when the soldier is reminded of the death of a friend. As the Army routinely remembers its dead, such a situation is unavoidable. What becomes more problematic is when a soldier is reminded about his friend's death every time another soldier, one he may not know, is killed in combat. Such information, rightly reported on the news, has an unforeseen impact on those still grieving. It is as if the soldier's grief is reawakened, like a wound that fails to heal. Soldiers' experience seems to be that each time this happens it is less distressing, until they get to a point where they do not 'overreact' at all.

Perhaps inevitably the Army chaplain becomes a 'death special-ist'. In an organization that is trained to kill, the death of another soldier is rarely anticipated and always difficult. During my ministry, I have spent more time with those who are dead, dying or grieving than have the great majority of soldiers and officers. It is this experience that allows a chaplain to appear calm at a point when many are not. Furthermore, it is important to recognize that at the point of death there is little anyone else can do. It is at this point, in this sad moment, that eyes turn to the chaplain and a soul is commended to God. As previously discussed, this simple act, in words and ritual, is very precious. While we fulfil many roles for the soldiers, this specialist care at the point of death is unique and greatly valued.

As I have considered these matters I have wondered whether other ministers experience the same situations as I do. I expect some of them are common to all forms of ministry. I was particularly interested to see some correlation with the emerging work of the disaster chaplains. Rabbi Stephen Roberts and the Revd William Ashley Sr comment in their book *Disaster Spiritual Care* that:

> It is often the simple presence of a person of God that provides healing and comfort. The ministry of solidarity and accompaniment, of silence in the face of tragedy, of surrender to the God of our understanding, is often the most we can do in such situations. (Roberts and Ashley, 2008, p. xviii)

This certainly resonates with my experience: a ministry of presence reflecting the incarnation of Christ among his people (cf. John 1.14). Furthermore I recognize that we have a similar understanding of silence: that in such situations silence is not an empty space, but a gift from God. I have been struck by the following advice given to the disaster chaplains. Chaplain Therese Becker, Greg Bodin and the Revd Arthur Schmidt suggest that in their context, 'Spiritual care is a painful accompaniment, a deep listening to the rawest expression of human suffering. It may or may not include prayer. It may or may not include words' (Roberts and Ashley, 2008, p. 92).

Once again this echoes my experience of public prayer at times of tragedy. As a minister trained in speaking and educated through books, words and essays, it is remarkable that not using these skills might quite often be the right path to tread. This feels counter-intuitive, but my experience tells me that sometimes words get in the way of what God is doing.

The key difference, as I discern it, is that disaster chaplaincy often occurs during a mass casualty scenario; whereas military chaplaincy now is more often concerned with smaller numbers.

The Army chaplains of the First World War were very aware of both accompanying their people through pain, and living with the reality of mass casualties. The famous advice given by the Revd Geoffrey Studdert Kennedy to the Revd Theodore Bayley Hardy VC, as he prepared to deploy to the front line, outlines this incarnational ministry:

> Live with the men, go everywhere they go. Make up your mind you will share all their risks, and more . . . Take a box of fags in your haversack, and a great deal of love in your heart and go up to them; laugh with them, joke with them. You can pray with them sometimes; but pray for them always!
>
> (Smyth, 1968, p. 175)

While I think it is unlikely I would ever offer soldiers cigarettes, the principles of our ministry have changed very little. I have often wondered how overwhelmed the chaplains of both world wars must have been, the human cost being so much greater than in our present conflicts. What we can certainly see is that chaplaincy in these extreme situations, particularly when people are grieving, is about walking the road with them, and sharing our faith and wisdom appropriately as we travel.

Finally, if you have got this far and you are still reading, then I urge you to pray for our servicemen and women. As combat operations in Afghanistan draw to a close, many will be living with the pain that the conflict has caused. I ask you to pray for peace so that our military forces are not needed, and to be patient with the thousands of veterans who have served in the military over the last ten years. They will live with these conflicts for the rest of their lives and we have a duty to care for them as far as we are able. I suspect that society will want to forget our recent controversial conflicts; the soldiers, however, will never be able to forget. They will need the support of their families, the government, society and – if we are willing – the Church.

References

Methodist Church of Great Britain (1999), 'Prayer with the Dying', in *Methodist Worship Book*, Peterborough: Methodist Publishing House.

Roberts, Rabbi Stephen B. and Ashley, Revd William W. C., Sr, eds (2008), *Disaster Spiritual Care: Practical Clergy Responses to Community, Regional and National Tragedy*, Woodstock, VT: SkyLight Paths Publishing.

Smyth, John (1968), *In This Sign Conquer*, London: Mowbray.